RIVERS RUN

By the same author:
The Idle Angler
The Twitch

RIVERS
RUN

An angler's journey from source to sea

KEVIN PARR

LONDON • SYDNEY • AUCKLAND • JOHANNESBURG

10 9 8 7 6 5 4 3 2 1

Rider, an imprint of Ebury Publishing,
20 Vauxhall Bridge Road,
London SW1V 2SA

Rider is part of the Penguin Random House group of companies
whose addresses can be found at global.penguinrandomhouse.com

Penguin
Random House
UK

First published by Rider in 2016

www.penguin.co.uk

A CIP catalogue record for this book is available from the British
Library

ISBN 9781846044915

Printed and bound in Great Britain by Clays Ltd, St Ives PLC

MIX
Paper from
responsible sources
FSC® C018179

Penguin Random House is committed to a sustainable future for
our business, our readers and our planet. This book is made from
Forest Stewardship Council® certified paper.

And if the river should ever run dry,
Somewhere the rain will still fall from the sky

Karine Polwart, 'Rivers Run'

To my wife, Sue

CONTENTS

A Note about the Text

Over the following pages you may notice that I refer to anglers in the masculine. This is purely for ease of flow – 'fisherman' rolls more smoothly off the tongue than 'fisherperson'; while for every 'he', I really mean 'he or she' – but the former is simpler to use in the text. Although angling is male-dominated, some of the very finest fisherfolk have been female. In fact, the British record salmon and the biggest ever fly-caught salmon were both famously caught by women. Therefore, before anyone thinks I might be mildly misogynistic, please be assured to the contrary!

Also, I often refer to rivers as feminine. However, this is less about narrative flow and more to do with a personal feeling. While I do not regard every river as female, some, such as the Kennet and Itchen, have an almost indiscernible quality that 'feels' far more female than male – certainly to me at least. Interestingly, in the German language, where nouns are defined as either masculine, feminine or neuter (der, die and das), the majority of rivers are prefaced by 'die': female. And while I could never get to grips with gender in my German classes at school, that distinction certainly makes sense to me now.

I

BEGINNINGS

Return to Stourhead

I am thankful for the breeze. This morning's haze dissolved as soon as I dropped down from the hills and here the sky is clear and the sun relentless above the shingle. I lay down my rod and kick off my flip-flops, giving the sea a quick toe-test before sitting back on the pebbles. The water is cool but not cold, the flooding tide warming over sun-baked stones.

There is an irresistible excitement when fishing a water for the first time. That first cast into the unknown, where absolutely anything could happen. In the past, I would have rushed to set up a rod, believing that the only way to catch a fish is to get a line in the water at the soonest opportunity. Experience, though, has taught me otherwise. Far more can be learned by not casting – by sitting, breathing and sharing the rhythm of the water. There are subtleties that can only be noted through observation and absorption, and we see little if we don't give our eyes a chance to focus.

So, for now, I will just sit back and let my chest rise and fall, because today there is even more reason to slow down. This beach is not simply a new spot for me to fish; the sea itself represents a whole new world. I have dabbled in sea fishing in the past, from rocks and piers and the odd boat, but my first cast here symbolises a new life. Gone are the mortgage, the savings and the monthly pay packet. Circumstance and illness have led my wife, Sue, and me into a life of rural simplicity. We have little now, and gather our own wood for the fire and supplement our cupboards with free gifts from nature's larder. If I catch a fish or two this afternoon then they will be eaten for supper. Should I fail, we will not starve quite yet, but for the time being this is the only way we can afford to eat protein-rich food such as fish.

Considering my inexperience at this sort of fishing, I feel confident. There should be mackerel riding this flood, crashing into the flashing sparkle of whitebait shoals out there along the shore. I have visited other stretches of this coast and seen anglers lined up almost shoulder to shoulder from east to west. They thump out a team of feathers and winch them back with great sweeps of the rod, over and over, waiting for a shoal of mackerel to move through and dance on the end of their lines.

I have come away from the crowds for this, my first attempt. This beach might not be as well regarded as others but with no fellow anglers here, any fish that show will be mine alone to cast among. And it is for signs of fish that I am looking, shapes in the water or shadows in the surf – any nuance or anomaly that might lead me to mackerel. I will watch the gulls and terns and follow their gaze. This is a new language to me but one I am sure I can slowly decipher if I consider what I have already learned on my journey here. For the moment, however, it is a language that is but a whisper.

A flotilla of gulls, black-headed and herring, bob gently a hundred yards offshore, while a pair of crows sit silently on the shingle to my left. They are waiting as I am, and their presence reassures me that something will happen. I reach for a rod and slowly put it up, pausing as I thread each ring, scanning and listening. The mass of water before me has softened slightly, the surface appears less sharp, less impenetrable, perhaps responding to the warmth of the air and the gentle flood of the tide. My mind no longer swims as I consider the enormity of the expanse, and instead, as I become less daunted, I find small pockets of familiarity. The sea might be vast – and salty – but ultimately I am just a little bit further down the river than I've been before. It is feasible that I have encountered this water before – odd particles of it at least. Perhaps flowing through the Dorset Stour at the end of last season. Maybe in the Hampshire Avon the summer before, or in the Kennet two winters ago. The drop that is still glistening on my toenail might have flowed in the Thames once, or along a tiny Highland stream where I've caught brown trout.

And now it is evaporating, heading skyward with a billion other droplets, massing together only to drop once more.

I wonder where it will fall. Somewhere far out over the sea, or perhaps inland – deep inland. It might sink through the surface strata and bubble up back at the beginning, at the very start of the stream. I feel an urge to return upstream myself and retread the path that has led me here, to revisit those places that helped shape me as an angler and a person. But how would it feel to go back?

I've threaded the rod but not yet tied on a lure. For some minutes I have been holding the tag end of the line between the fingers of my left hand and flicking it with the thumb of my other. I could start my journey right now – chuck the rod back in the boot and point the car north. There is time today, though it would mean missing out on our fish supper.

As I ponder, a gull's chatter catches my attention. Wings are spread and in seconds the bobbing flotilla has become an airborne squadron. The crows hop up and glide with purpose past my nose. Something is happening. I reach for my binoculars and look to where the birds are flying. A few hundred yards to the west, on the very edge of the shore, is a shower of glass. Thousands of tiny fish desperately leaping from hungry mouths. The surface boils like a puddle in a hailstorm, followed by bigger splashes as the mackerel throw themselves into the shoal. I reach for a lure; I will venture back upstream, but not just yet.

In the south-west corner of Wiltshire, just a short hop from Somerset and Dorset, sits a tiny pool. It is no bigger than a puddle and, but for the boot-clinging squelch surrounding it, I could probably jump both its length and breadth. It is shallow and clear yet teeming with life. Dozens of midge larvae hang from the surface film, while between them flit water boatmen no bigger than grains of rice. The margins beside my feet are blanketed by ivy-leaved crowfoot whose watercress-green leaves contrast with the mauve stems of water purslane. A tiny water beetle breaks surface, conspicuous as he sinks from the ball-bearing bubble of air he carries on his tail.

There is always water here and I don't need to see the steady streams of bubbles rising from the bottom of the pool to know this. This seemingly insignificant splash of water is the source of the Dorset Stour, a river as rich in life as it is in form, and with whose banks I have become familiar in recent years. I first fished her when I was ten or eleven years old. At the time, I was visiting my best friend in the world, Ian Murray, whose family had moved him to the other end of the earth – although we would still see one another during school holidays. Fishing was more my thing than his, but Ian had a rod and reel, and the Stour flowed through Sturminster Newton where he went to school, so we had to fish it. His mother dropped us off at Fiddleford Mill a mile or two downstream from Sturminster, a small market town and ancient fording point on the Stour, where Thomas Hardy lived when he wrote of the sorrows of Clym Yeobright in *The Return of the Native*.

Within minutes of our arrival, the rain began to fall, and after an hour of tangled lines and motionless floats, a man in a green wax jacket and matching hat wandered down the bank and asked to see our permits. Ian and I looked at one another in panic. We hadn't even thought of the need for permission. Ian mumbled something about his mother forgetting to pick them up and the grown-up nodded and half smiled. He might have confiscated our tackle, but instead he pointed us to the other side of the weir pool where some chub might be lying under the trailing branches of a willow. We didn't catch any, but my first-ever minnow saved a blank, and we were so sodden that we were packed up and ready to go long before Ian's mother arrived to rescue us.

More than a decade was to pass before I returned to the Stour, although I soon became well aware of her pedigree. Not long after my trip with Ian, one of the angling newspapers led with the tale of a 'Giant Dorset Stour Roach'. The story had quite an impact on me. Despite not knowing exactly where the roach was caught, I felt that I had had a brush with something extraordinary.

Today, as a recently adopted Dorsetphile myself, I fish the Stour's middle reaches throughout the winter and on occasion she is generous with her rewards. While she can be fickle, and bursts her banks angrily after prolonged rain, few rivers share her intrigue and subtle changes of character. I would never profess to know her well – certainly there are other rivers with whom I am far better acquainted – but I know enough of her to be struck curious by her beginnings.

Now, a short distance behind me – forty-seven paces to be precise – stands a monument placed to mark the river's rising. It is a curious structure. Beneath a short, tapered spire sit six figures, each within a curved recess that make up the sides of a hexagon. Beneath each corner is a pillar, the six of which sit upon a large square plinth. The base of the structure is far less defined – a misshapen hedgehog mound of rock which is tangled with the spines of bramble. At its base is the clue to the structure's original purpose: a small bowl into which would once have bubbled freshwater from a spring below. The monument is well weathered, having stood here for nearly 250 years, before which it served as a functional water source in the city of Bristol.

In 1768, when Henry Hoare had St Peter's Pump relocated from the city and rebuilt upon this rural site, he was unlikely to have known that its intended role might lack permanence. He had planned to place the monument upon the very spot, or at least the closest spot with suitable foundations, where the river that formed the centrepiece to his estate first appeared. To this day, Stourhead is known as the source of the River Stour – and yet St Peter's Pump is in the wrong place. Not simply because the water table has shifted and there is only ever flowing water here in the wettest of winters, but because the river has never truly begun here.

Although most visitors to the Stourhead estate, and there are many, will be aware of the symbolic significance of this place, a stranger walking through this valley would most likely look at the monument and see a simple folly – which in some respects is exactly what it is. While a spring still pushes a tiny pool above the ground here, there is no flow from it. A short run of club rushes alludes to the water's initial movement, but these quickly fizzle into nothing and for some distance there is only grass. The steadily sinking water table has forced the water-course back beneath the ground and while the rushes do eventually find sufficient water to take root once more, these are hundreds of yards distant.

Far more prominent is the needle-straight path worn by a thousand soles into the side of the eastern slope, which caught my eye earlier when I first stepped out upon the head of the valley. From that vantage point, the rush-lined river course is slightly more obvious as it is gently concertinaed by the foreshortened aspect. I stood there for some minutes, silently taking in the scene before me and soothed by the warm southerly breeze that brushed my face and whispered in waves through the beech trees behind me. The valley was deeper than I had expected and almost glacial in appearance. Carved out, perhaps, by a giant with an enormous ice-cream scoop. A solitary oak with bark like a crocodile's back was the only tree that appeared not to have been deliberately planted, and although I am no great fan of manicured landscape, there was enough scrub and general untidiness to hold my interest. I ignored the well-trodden path and walked straight down towards the monument itself, putting up meadow pipits as I strode, and snaffling blackberries as I gently zigzagged between brambles to the place where I find myself now.

It is early October, yet summer lingers over the landscape. After an arid, record-breaking warm September, the ground is hard and dusty, and the only signs of moisture are the squelchy patch of bog in which I now stand and the microcosm of freshwater in front of my toes. I opt not to follow the course of club rush south into the trees. Most likely I will find no flowing water before reaching the chain of ornamental lakes that this spring feeds, and, having spent so many hours fishing beside the Stour, I prefer to look upon its uppermost reaches as a small bubble of possibility rather than a man-made curio. Instead, I cross to sit in the shade of an enormous birch tree to the west of the monument, where I eat my packed lunch as the seeps and pipes of goldcrests fill the pine trees behind me. I am grateful to be out of the sun and content to keep my own company. A young couple has decided to take their own lunch beside the monument and I happily let them enjoy the space. The man sets down a toddler from a harness on his back and the child is off like a rocket, running excitedly round the blackberry-stained stones, a clockwork toy finally allowed to spin.

I should have come here in spring – when the world was waking up. It would have been a more appropriate season in which to gauge a sense of the river's beginning. The swallows would be hawking up the valley, picking off flies before arrowing over the beech trees and on to who knows where. The beeches themselves would be bare, save those stubborn few brown leaves that seem to forget they are supposed to fall. Today, the beeches are still dressed in a green almost as deep as they would have worn in late May, but when they do turn it will be sudden and potentially stunning.

With a satisfied sigh, I turn my face towards the autumn sun. Still the toddler runs, oblivious to the season or the significance of the spot where his feet pad. He is suitably enthusiastic, full of the hope and possibility to be found within the water bubbling up beneath him. I wonder if the toddler might one day fish – if he will find himself as captivated by water as I am. Today might be significant in the toddler's life, yet he will most likely not recall it. The smells and warmth and space will filter into his subconscious and maybe rise in a future bolt of pleasure. Alternatively, he might nosedive into the squelchy pool and get a mouthful of Stour that will put him off water for life.

— 🖋 —

I was little older than that toddler and had barely got to grips with the fact that fleas jump and birds fly, when I first became aware of the world that exists beneath water. I suddenly had to comprehend a place that didn't have a bottom and that you couldn't touch without getting wet, yet things actually lived within it. My godfather owned a garden centre on the outskirts of Basingstoke, long since bulldozed and swallowed up by sprawl, where he kept an array of ponds and water features that I would gaze into for hours. Goldfish were the obvious reward, easy to spot even among the weeds. Then there were the water snails, the pond skaters and water boatmen, and in spring the amphibians would poke out their noses. The more I looked the more I saw, but it was always the fish that mesmerised me. They seemed to glide through the water far more easily than birds flapped through the air. They would hang mid-depth, not stirring a fin, before the slightest tremor would ease them out of sight. They were completely unlike anything I had encountered in the dry world, but I didn't feel any urge to catch them – to make them real. Not straight away.

My father was an angler and, when he realised I was interested, began to point out different species of fish in different places: the carp cutting lines across the surface of Alresford Pond and the mullet skulking around the keels in the marina at Hamble. Similarly, my grandfather was always happy to accompany me down to the riverside when holidaying with us on the edge of Dartmoor.

My memories of him are scented with the tobacco smoke that kept the air around us insect-free. Although I had no idea at the time, one reason why Grandad was always happy to take us to the river was so that he could sneak an extra pinch of tobacco without my grandmother raising an eyebrow.

My brother Richard and I, and occasionally my sister, Catherine, would sit on the rocks just below a bend where the current slowed to form a deep, lazy pool. Sometimes just one or two fish would rise, but when the air was thick with fly-life the trout would hurl themselves about with abandon. A few of the fish were large, even as I look back with adult eyes, and to a young child they were gargantuan. Yet from my low vantage point the surface of that pool on the River Teign looked impenetrable – like a vast sheet of aluminium foil. The insects that dropped onto it did not pass through and instead sent out tiny ripples that made the reflections shimmer. Only the fish could break through the film, and they needed violence to do so. I still remember the sound of their splashes almost as clearly as the sweet smell of my grandfather's pipe.

For young eyes, the trout that swim within clear waters are perfect subjects. They are reliable, holding station in the same spot day after day, but more importantly they will come and join our world. In late May, chalk-stream fly fishing becomes temporarily straightforward as the air fills with mayfly. Some anglers call it 'duffers fortnight', for as the clouds of insects fill the skies the trout go into a feeding frenzy. Even the least competent caster can catch with a mayfly imitation during these couple of weeks – even a duffer like me. And it is not only the fish that enjoy the feast. Grey wagtails fling themselves into the midst of the mass while higher fly the hirundines: swallows and martins, some still fresh from Africa, all lost within the gorge of the glut. Hobbies dive among them with shared intent. And though they shadow and prey upon the hirundines throughout the rest of the year, the hobbies care only for mayfly when the hatch is on. It is, after all, far easier to catch a meal that can be eaten on the wing than one that requires plucking.

Perhaps because of their sheer numbers when they emerge, we know the mayfly almost solely for the last throes of its life, yet theirs is an extraordinary process. They hatch from the water with no mouth and a digestive system containing nothing but the air needed to aid flight; and they require a further moult in order to reach sexual maturity. All this occurs in a matter of hours – and yet the mayfly naiad or nymph has already lived beneath the surface of the water for a year or more. Of course, when mayflies were first observed by early man their entire life-cycle could not possibly have been understood. The mayfly's seemingly ephemeral life would have been perceived as simply that. Lasting just a day. Yet, even with our improved knowledge, we struggle to see beyond the winged insect and consider its life within the water.

The surface of the smallest watercourse acts like a barrier to us, and our recognition of a species such as this one is affected by which side of the veil it is encountered. We have a similar attitude to most metamorphic life, although many life-cycles are more easily defined because they occur solely on one side of the watery divide. It is when the edges blur that we struggle to understand them. Beginnings, it seems, remain elusive: is it ever possible to pin them down?

— ❧ —

The true source of a river is similarly ambiguous. The water that rises near to where I am sitting has come from somewhere else – from underground. Furthermore, that subterranean source has been fed by water seeping down into the earth through precipitation. This, as we all learn at school, is part of the Water Cycle, an ever-rotating process. Evaporation, condensation, infiltration – terms that will still be familiar to many of us from geography lessons – and yet, despite the perpetuity of the process, surely a river's source should represent more than an indefinable point within a circle?

As I wash down my lunch with a glug of water from my flask, I turn my attention once more to the monument nearby and smile. On the one hand there is the apparent absurdity of Henry Hoare's whim – transporting a relic brick by brick in order to mark something that doesn't really exist. On the other hand, however, I rather like the notion. It demonstrates the respect and appreciation that Hoare had for the river that landscaped his home (along with the well-honed skill of Capability Brown). A river deserves our respect after all. In fact, one only needs to look downstream on a map to see the impact that the Stour has had throughout its length: Milton on Stour, East Stour, Stour Provost, Sturminster Newton – I could cast my way through countless villages, towns and watermills that owe their existence to this one river. And when I came to this place this morning I had planned to do just that. Not in a day, of course, but over time I had thought to explore wherever I wouldn't be trespassing and to cast wherever I was able.

I realise there is a different path I must follow. This entails not a simple exploration of a single river, or the fish I might catch from it, but an understanding of what it is that makes someone an angler – what it is that makes me an angler. This is about the landscape and environment within which I immerse myself and of which I so often feel a part. It is about the ways we interact with our surroundings, and what they tell us about ourselves. Although I don't always need a rod in my hand to feel as though I belong by the waterside, it was angling that helped open my eyes. And as I sit here, I can hear the river calling me, bubbling up from deep underground, sharing its secrets.

2

TURNING STONES

A tributary of the Exe

As last summer faded into autumn, my sister Catherine and her family spent a weekend camping on the coast in the hamlet of Eype, not far from our cottage. The first night was chilly, but the following dawn broke with hazy sunshine and by the time I joined them for lunch the day was soft and warm.

After lunch, we decided to amble along the cliff path, down to the sea. When we reached the beach, Bertie and Bader, my nephew and niece, had their attention snatched. A small wooden footbridge straddled a slip of water that was significant enough to have cut a course for itself through the rocks over the millennia, but so tame after a dry summer that it disappeared into the shingle before reaching the sea. Immediately below the bridge, however, the trickle of water slid out across a lump of bedrock to form an ankle-deep pool.

To a five- and three-year-old, this place was heaven, and they were not the only ones to think so. Half a dozen kids were paddling and splashing in the fresh water, seemingly oblivious to the vast sea that rattled the pebbles just seventy yards away. While the lack of sand that typifies this stretch of Jurassic coast might affect a small child's perception of what a beach is, these children played in the stream as if there were nowhere else in the world they'd rather be. It was curious to watch. The toddler who had run around St Peter's Pump at Stourhead was too young to even notice the presence of water nearby, while my niece and nephew, just a year or two older, were more aware, but also limited by their capacity. The water here was clean and clear and safe to engage with. There might be life in there, somewhere, but all these children cared for was to touch, feel and understand the water itself. Nearby, on the pebbles of the beach, parents sat in the sunshine, some even venturing into the waves, but for their offspring the sea could wait.

It seemed rather apt that the Eype stream should choose at the last to slow right down. Having rushed excitedly down the valley like a puppy on a short lead, it suddenly found that its journey was all too short. As the air began to be tainted with the spray of salt from the sea, the stream began to dawdle. Until this point, its course had been dark and hidden, trickling through a deep gully in the bedrock – narrow and overhung by brambles and ferns that all but hide its very existence. 'Hang on ...' it seemed to beg, forming a final defiant pool before slipping into the shingle.

It was natural that Bertie, Bader and the rest of the children should find contentment here. Water is a substance that forms us and yet as adults we often feel averse to it: we are dependent upon it, yet aware it can take a life in a moment; we harness it for power and industry, knowing it may grow angry and break its shackles as swiftly as rain clouds roll across the sky. However, as children, our curiosity normally outweighs our wariness and long before we begin to consider water as a habitat for other life forms we become captured by its movement and the feel of it. We don't care whether there are fish or caddis larvae or water beetles in it; for now, water simply needs to be accessible. And here, at Eype, the water was clean and clear and the bottom of the stream firm.

While Bader was content to paddle, Bertie soon discovered further attractions. He realised how a small piece of driftwood could deflect the current, whereas bigger stones would slow the flow to a crawl. In these last days of summer, he still thought of water primarily as something to dam or fill buckets, but before winter came, Bertie was to catch his first fish on rod and line.

The evolution of an angler is similar. As his relationship with water develops and he is driven to connect with the life he has discovered within it, he does so with minimal fuss. At first, there is no time to spend mulling over which rod or net to use: the urge to connect is far more simplistic. As he has discovered water through touch, so he must build upon his understanding in the same manner, feeling his way bit by bit.

As I reflect upon my own path, I know that I must leave my fishing rod in its bag for a little while longer. It's time to get my hands dirty.

— ⊸ —

I'm heading west. Well, north-west really, but the latter part of this journey would have looked horizontal on a map. It is many years since I travelled along this road, but I nevertheless expected it to be more familiar. Instead, vast stretches are avenued by dense beech hedge, the top branches of which have sprouted many feet skyward, shielding the rolls of north Somerset from this motorist's view. I'm sure there are fewer accidents as a result, and the local barn owls can now cross the road at a safer height, but the tight lines seem rather clinical. Having not set foot on Exmoor for more years than I can remember, I'd rather hoped to see more of it.

Our family holidays almost always headed towards the setting sun. My parents were both teachers and, although this meant we were unable to afford the exotic trips that some of my classmates enjoyed, we were blessed with time. Holidays involved moorland, mountains and wooded valleys, and I couldn't have been happier.

My interest for the natural world has always extended beyond the sub-aqua, and, as a child, birds were my great love. Though my passion was for all things feathered, raptors soared highest in my thoughts. My childhood home in rural Hampshire was not especially recognised for birds of prey. Kestrels nested locally and were still common, while the occasional sparrow hawk would blur through the garden. But that was pretty much it. There were owls – barn, tawny and little were all regularly spotted, but to see anything else required a visit to the New Forest or further afield.

After heavy persecution and widespread use of insecticides such as DDT, by the mid-twentieth century birds such as the peregrine, buzzard, raven and hen harrier had been driven to the far west and north of the British Isles. Here they found refuge in the more rugged and wild folds of our landscape. Out of sight but not entirely out of mind. As populations tumbled, so their eggs became more highly prized. The red kite numbered only a handful of pairs in mid-Wales and yet these birds were hounded by collectors. Such was the mentality of these individuals that the kites were disturbed throughout the breeding season and their nests often destroyed, meaning that, for the collectors, an intact British egg remained highly unusual and highly prized.

Fortunately, improvements in the protection and understanding of these birds have led to the recovery of many of our raptor species. The Welsh population of red kites has been supplemented nationally by a reintro-duction programme and the species is now flourishing. The buzzard has become our most common bird of prey, and, despite its relative profligacy, my heart still soars whenever I see one. They are common around the hills of our West Dorset home; in fact, a couple of years ago I counted twenty-seven on a single thermal. But when I was a child, their distribution was still limited and it was only during holidays that I might hope to glimpse one.

In the south-west of England, where my family often ventured, buzzards maintained a steady population through the heaviest years of persecution. The landscape, dominated by Dartmoor, Exmoor and Bodmin Moor, was unsuited to widespread arable use and, if farmed at all, would be used for the grazing of hardy sheep and cattle. With conservation-minded forestry also widespread, these areas, though not particularly forgiving, were at least reasonably safe havens.

Dartmoor became the most familiar area to me of the three moorlands, although we stayed mainly on its fringes, where my grandfather's pipe smoke swirled in the calm air of the Teign Valley. In contrast, the high moor could seem bleak and unwelcoming, particularly in poor weather. The presence of the MOD may also have been a factor, but more imposing were the treeless hills topped with crops of granite. These tors are found on Bodmin Moor as well, as both areas were formed in the Permian Period, some 300 million years ago, from the granite intrusion known as the Cornubian batholith. With their similar geology, Bodmin and Dartmoor may, on occasion, have an aura of desolation. Both rise from the surrounding farmland and wooded river valleys in great blisters of rock. These places are imposing and ruthless – and inspire dark tales of smuggling, wrecking and great howling hounds.

In contrast, Exmoor offers a softer intimacy. Here, a more diverse geological make-up has created a wider range of habitat and landscape. As a specific area, Exmoor seems less naturally defined than the other two moorlands do. The landscape gently rolls upwards from the river valleys, the river water carving more deeply into the soft sedimentary rock than the granite-herded streams of Dartmoor can. The moor itself is a typical upland habitat, and still holds small populations of birds that one might not expect to find in southern Britain. Ring ouzel and merlin are clinging on in the area, although the red grouse has now likely vanished as a breeding bird.

In the centre of Exmoor lies Exford, a small village whose two hotels are reminders of a time when much of the surrounding area was royal hunting forest. Tourists still fill the hotel rooms, along with the occasional angler looking to find sparkling trout in the Upper Exe or one of the smaller tributaries. The village church sits on the eastern edge of the village and beside it is the lay-by in which I now sit. The village hasn't changed much since I was a child and I'm filled with the pleasant glow of familiarity after miles of cold, beech-shrouded confusion. It should be no surprise that the churchyard has altered little during the thirty-odd years that have passed since I was last here, but the pathway running alongside it has me puzzled. There is a gate now and vehicular access down to the cottage where we once used to stay. Behind the church is a cricket clubhouse that certainly wasn't there when I last visited; but time and weather have softened sharp edges and it is impossible to identify what is truly different and what I have simply forgotten.

As I drop down the slope the cottage comes into view. The current owners might be able to drive down to it now that the track has been improved, and although the solar panels on the roof look to have been replaced since I was last here, the garden still melds into the surrounding landscape. The building had been recently renovated when we first stayed here all those years ago, and the work had given the place a peculiar smell: that deep evocative mustiness so typical of older buildings, but with an underlying mortar tone – a concrete tinge that seemed to stick in your nose much like the dust billowing from the back of a combine harvester.

In those days, the electricity in Gunns Cottage came solely from the roof panels, while water was drained directly into the house from the small stream that burbled down through the garden. With barely enough power to spark a couple of light bulbs we spent most of our time in candlelight, reading or playing cards. There was no television and no radio, just the hiss and crackle of the fire and the whisper of water sliding across the pebbles in the stream outside. It was paradise.

The stream was the immediate and most obvious attraction for me and my two siblings. On our first visit, a fish spooked from the wide water near the ford where our own little stream had joined another on their way to the Exe. We had not brought rods and, in truth, my brother and I were still a year or two away from comfortably wielding one, but as we climbed up the incline to the cottage we realised that the ever-diminishing trickle was probably too small for fish. It didn't matter, though: it was *our* water and it had to be explored.

The best and often the only way to explore small streams is to get into the water. Often the course is overgrown and untrodden – a small ribbon of wild cutting through a managed world. This stretch of water was no different, cutting a channel through an eye-scratching mass of hawthorn and bramble. Occasionally it would drop or twist, pausing just long enough to bore out a hole deeper than our wellies were high. We were tackling the Amazon rainforest. This was uncharted territory in which fifty yards took well over half an hour to negotiate.

As the undergrowth on the east bank began to thin, so a steady slope drew my interest upwards. A damp ditch led up to an ash tree beside a gap in the stone wall, which in turn obscured the view beyond. I needed to see what the ash tree saw. We split three ways. Catherine went back to the cottage, Richard pressed on upstream into the pine woods, while I climbed into the open. I was to be gone for a good few hours.

I kept my gaze low as I walked, keen to wait until I was beside the ash tree before I took in the view. At the moment that I approached the gap, the mew of a buzzard rang across the valley. I turned and picked the bird out immediately, gliding low across the tops of the pine trees. Perhaps I had disturbed it – or perhaps it was simply announcing its arrival to a mate. The buzzard turned, flapped twice and then stretched its wings into a 'V' as it found some lift and began to soar.

I raced up the final few yards and dropped beside the trunk of the tree, shuffling backwards until I was sitting flush against the bark. Before me was the sweep of pine trees that followed the path of the stream down from the head of the valley. The field in front of the trees was speckled with gorse and grazed by sheep – and looks just the same today.

Thirty years later, I sit down in the very same spot, having skirted the garden via a footpath and crossed a style at the foot of the hill. I am a little more aware of where my backside is resting than when I first sat here, but finding the curve of the trunk just as obliging. There are sheep grazing but no sign of any buzzards, as the low cloud and light drizzle will keep them grounded unless they absolutely have to fly.

That first time, I stayed here until I knew my mother would start fretting. There were soon two buzzards above the pines – obviously a pair and obviously, even to my inexperienced eyes, nesting in the pine trees below. I couldn't tell precisely where, but I didn't care too much. It was enough for me to know that our holiday cottage lay within a few wing beats of my favourite birds. Over the next few days I would scoot up to see *my* buzzards whenever I could. I was developing a serious raptor fixation, but there were other distractions. Damming work had begun on the stream in the garden and as a result Richard had made a stunning discovery.

— ◂ —

The Parr Bros (and Sister) Damming Company were prolific barrier builders in the late seventies and early eighties. Like many children, wherever we found running water we would also find a reason to slow down the flow, even if our efforts were highly temporary. Success would depend upon the flow and the material available, with the Welsh Mountains perhaps offering the pick of the rocks even if the steep slopes made construction tricky. On a beach near St Ives in Cornwall, a lovely wide slither of water became a pool almost deep enough to swim in. We couldn't find many rocks to work with, but the sand seemed to stick together like wet snow and, perhaps more vitally, we were assisted by a small army of strangers desperate to get involved in our construction work. A horde of children can achieve much if sharing a vision – and this one was a dam worthy of Herbert Hoover.

Here, at Gunns Cottage on Exmoor, there was scope for more extensive work.

When I returned after that first buzzard encounter, Richard and Catherine were already busy building in the stream. The flow was moderate and, as the stream had a stone bed, there was plenty of material to work with, but I was too late to get very involved that first evening.

As our mother called us for the third time to sit up to table, Richard jumped with surprise.

'A fish!' he exclaimed.

I hurried over but he was already looking blankly around his feet.

'A trout?' I asked.

'Not sure ... it wasn't big, but it was really quick!'

I woke early the next morning, sparked to life by the sound of running water. The same music that had soothed me into a deep sleep in the darkness of the previous evening now called to me with a distinct urgency. The glistening water was more welcoming, and seemed almost to sing in the early morning sun.

I hadn't considered how I might catch the fish, or even whether it was my intention to do so. What I needed first was to prove the fish's existence. Somewhat surprisingly, this didn't take that long. I slipped into the water at the point of yesterday's sighting and worked slowly upstream, with my back arched and my hands clasped behind my back.

My young eyes were sharp but the real advantage of childhood is a proximity to the ground. These days, as I creep around the local woods in autumn with a mushroom basket on my arm, my back bears the brunt as I stoop ever closer to the forest floor. If I stand up straight, my eyes are nearly six feet above the soles of my boots and spotting a fungal-shaped anomaly among the random scattering of curled fallen leaves is tricky from such a height. It's all about getting your eye in, of course – spot a single *Cantharellus tubaeformis* and suddenly you'll see a hundred – but mushroom picking would be far easier with young eyes and half the height.

In that Exmoor stream, my eyes were so busy scanning the water ahead of me that I failed to notice when the toe of my boot inched beneath the edge of a large, dark rock. As I moved my foot, the stone shifted; a small cloud of grit billowed into the current and a dark-coloured fish flicked a tail upstream. The fish was slightly in the periphery of my vision, but I can picture it even now. My pulse quickened and I focused on the stone a step or two away from me where the fish had dematerialised. It had to be underneath the rock.

Like many children, I was well practised in the careful turning of stones in shallow water. Rock-pooling was an essential seaside activity, and even on sandy beaches I learned that a solitary stone in the shallows could hide a surprise or two. The key was to lift it slowly, with minimal disturbance to the sand. With a little care and a slice of good fortune, whatever might be hiding beneath the stone would sit there, momentarily at least, after their roof had been removed. Crabs were the most likely residents, or shrimps, but fish were the greatest prize.

There are plenty of species that spend their life in the pools and shallows of our inshore waters – and the finest find for a young rock pooler is surely the butterfish. Unlike some of the other fish that they rub fins with, butterfish do not sport spines or rows of needle-sharp teeth. Instead, they are long and slippery, with a row of black spots along their backs that are ringed with white and look like huge eyes. Their slim bodies enable them to find sanctuary in the tiniest of gaps, and even a fist-sized stone is sufficient to hide a fish of several inches.

One summer, I found a butterfish on a beach on Arran, in the west of Scotland, and was so proud of it that I took it back with me to the cottage where we were staying. It was a typical specimen, six or seven inches long. Not understanding why my parents thought the idea wrong, I snuck it into a small bucket of sea water and left it outside overnight. In the morning, it was very dead and the water stank like a fishing harbour on a hot day. It was a tough lesson learned; and if I were to catch the fish hiding in the stream of Gunns Cottage then I had already decided that it would not be kept out of the water any longer than it took my father to tell me what it was.

I eased up the rock and paused as the sediment beneath rose and resettled. There it was! A strange little brown curl of fish. It seemed oblivious to my threat and I simply picked it up with my free hand. It wriggled but not with any real purpose, and I ran up the garden with my prize. It looked like a goby – a fish I'd encountered in rock pools – with a huge head tapering down the body to the point of its tail. The fins and tail were folded flat but the pectoral fins were fanned out like a proud-plumed peacock and exaggerated the fish's triangular form.

My dad nodded as soon as he saw it. 'A miller's thumb,' he proclaimed before suggesting it would be better off in the water. I was reluctant to let it go, but Richard and Catherine had an alternative. Their morning's dam-building upstream had created a pool that would make a perfect home. The miller's thumb seemed to approve and quickly slipped out of sight between the stones on the bottom.

— ⋘ —

The miller's thumb, or bullhead as it is more commonly known, is not a fish that anglers would specifically target. It is widespread, growing no bigger than an ounce in weight and a few inches in length. I have caught many over the years, but none by design. Bullheads feed on small crustaceans and invertebrates, and a maggot or two on a hook makes a perfect dinner for them. They are typically found in small streams or the upper reaches of rivers, but can also be found throughout some river systems. Should a bullhead take your bait, he is unlikely to tell you about it. They usually sit tight and there is no tell-tale dip of a float or tweak of the line. Instead, you reel in to find a small brown blob dangling there, looking a little sorry for itself. They tend to stay completely still even while being unhooked, but invariably swim off with no ill effects.

Although my captures are occasional, my friend Martin Stevens is a reluctant expert. On a run of visits we made to the Kennet in search of barbel, he caught nothing but bullheads, and on one afternoon managed a triple brace. He didn't seem to be too proud of his achievement, and my gentle ribbing didn't help matters.

That said, I once caught a bullhead in Alresford Pond in Hampshire, which, although it is chalk-stream fed, is a large, silty water where such a fish seems altogether alien. They are best suited to small shallow streams where they swim near the top of the food chain. In those locations, the water is too cold and shallow for pike and perch to prowl, and the trout are so small that they are the bullhead's competitor rather than predator. Instead, the main threat comes from land or air. An otter or an errant mink might venture upstream, while herons, kingfishers and in more recent years little egrets will all make a meal of a bullhead.

The spread of the little egret into Britain has been dramatic. An occasional visitor thirty years ago, egrets first bred here in 1996 and now number in their thousands. In winter, they spread well inland and even in the valley below our Dorset cottage there are four or five birds present each winter. There, on the tiny River Wyn, they find sufficient food all through the cold months.

When we first moved to Dorset, I waded up a section of the Wyn – a tributary of the Hooke and in turn the

Frome, which is only a couple of miles long. I was sure the habitat would be perfect for bullheads and maybe loach, but saw none; yet there are obviously many present or the egrets would look elsewhere for food. Perhaps my bullhead-spotting skills have grown a little rusty, and I certainly did not search the Wyn with the same meticulous effort that I put in as a small boy in that little Exmoor stream.

I smile to myself as I stand up from my seat by the ash tree. I may have found nothing in the Wyn but surely I would here. Of course, I can no longer retrace my steps through the cottage garden, at least not without disturbing the current occupants, so instead I head up into the pine trees before slipping into the stream. It's cold and my toes curl away from the walls of my wellies as I work upstream. I find a tiny, inch-long trout in a slack, but soon realise that the water here tumbles too sharply to home a bullhead. I may have more chance below the cottage.

I return to the ford where the two streams meet, and in the pool below a dark shape shoots away under the bank. A bullhead. Had to be. And a big one too – though I won't be able to get to his hiding place. Instead I turn and head up the other stream that meets at this fork. The banks are high but it looks negotiable and within a minute I'm absorbed.

Although the surrounding area looks unchanged in some respects, it hasn't felt it; and during the course of my explorations so far I have felt distinctly underwhelmed. The new track down to the cottage has taken away its feeling of isolation and a small cluster of new houses has spoiled the view. Of course, it is possible that time has distorted my true memories of this place. What is without question, though, is that being here, in this overgrown stream, is like being in another world. Here, between the steep banks, beneath a canopy of small hedgerow trees, is a place where people do not usually tread. It is intense and intimate, and I like it.

I spot a big stone mid-stream about ten yards ahead. The water around it is steady and perhaps ten inches deep. There has to be a fish sheltering there.

I inch up and slowly, slowly lift the stone. Whoosh! A dark streak darts upstream and settles behind another rock five yards away. The spot is so overgrown that it is beyond my physical reach, although my eight-year-old self might have managed it. I could almost get there, but would have to lie flat in the water to pass under the hazel branches. I don't want to get wet and certainly don't need to. After all, I've made my memories real again, and these days I keep my feet dry and use a rod.

3

DIPPING A TOE

The Leidle

I got caught in a shower back in the autumn – a downpour really – while I was scouring the woods. I was without a jacket and would normally have sought shelter beneath a tree, but with my mushroom basket fairly full I opted to make a break for the car. I got soaked, and my jumper hung off me like a torn sail in a storm. As I sat in the driver's seat catching my breath and waiting for the mist to lift from my glasses, I caught a whiff that sent me spiralling. My jumper was wool, and for a moment its damp scent whisked me off to a Scottish mountainside, via the slightly malodorous funk of wet sheep.

Certain smells wedge themselves within our psyche, more deeply instilled than any sight or sound. We trust this sense as a result, and are happier to smell food to decide whether it is edible than rely on the way it looks. Smell, as with the other senses, is most acute when we are young, and this can be both a benefit and a disadvantage.

When I was five or six, I became poorly after eating smoked mackerel, and for years afterwards the slightest whiff would make my stomach turn somersaults. It's a sensible reaction really – my body was repulsing something that it had pretty good reason to believe was a poison. Today, after some careful conditioning in my late teens, I can enjoy smoked food without holding my nose, and there are some seemingly unpleasant smells that actually put me in a good place. Not just damp sheep, but the waft of sheep dung drying in the sun will see me floating off dreamily. Pine forest and heather are pleasant enough but chuck in a dash of pungent acid-laced bog and I'm in heaven.

Sometimes the journey of reminiscence is quite a long one. I might travel briefly to Devon, Wales or Cumbria, but ultimately every whiff of bracken or damp pine leads me to one particular place – the Isle of Mull.

On the way back from our first family holiday to Mull I stood on the stern of the ferry and cried as the island shrank in its wake. I couldn't believe anywhere on earth could be more perfect. My mum put her arm around me and promised that we would return. She was true to her word, and when we did we rediscovered a piece of heaven that would wedge itself into our souls forever.

My parents continued to return to Mull when we three kids were old enough to stay at home, and later so did we, when we realised there was more pleasure to be had in joining them in Scotland than sitting up late in a parent-free house. I have not been back to Mull every year – far from it – but have lost count of my visits there. Until today, though, I had never seen the island with her winter coat on.

— ✦ —

On my previous trip to Mull, it had been summer and my wife Sue had taken a photo from our bedroom window at twenty past eleven at night. The shot looked out to the south-west, across a flat mauve sea, and the light was still good enough to make out the ridges of rock on the Paps of Jura. I'd been up since five that morning, making the most of the day, and the sun was already warm when I first woke. The end of June is an astonishing time to be among the mountains and lochs of Scotland. In fact, were it not for the midges and the nibbling of the ticks acting as a steady reminder to the contrary, you could be forgiven for thinking you were in a dream.

Six months later in the year, in the week before Christmas, I find myself on a very different island. The journey to get here has been an adventure, with my friend Dan Kieran and I making a 1,200-mile round trip to enjoy a single full day on Mull. Our path has been littered with obstacles. A vicious storm has closed the railways, blocked roads and left Mull in candlelight. The long days of June seem impossibly distant. Darkness fell long before our four o'clock ferry delivered us yesterday and this morning's dawn did not flicker until well after we finished our breakfasts. We have come for the eagles and there is a small window of opportunity to spot them today. A lull between weather fronts, with another belt of snow due to sweep in from the west this afternoon.

— ◂━ —

For many anglers, winter is a time to hang up rods and warm toes by the fire. Some have no choice: during the winter months the rivers are off limits to anyone hoping to cast for salmon or sea trout – fish that as the days reach their shortest are busy digging redds in the riverbed in which to lay their eggs. The coarse fishing close season, a statutory lay-off period designed to protect spawning fish but now relaxed on still waters and some canals, runs later, from mid March until mid June, though many coarse anglers opt instead to take a winter break.

Cold weather can be quite a deterrent, particularly as the fish themselves often drift into torpor as temperatures plunge. Short days limit the opportunities for a cast outside of working hours, and the rivers themselves might be swollen by rain or numbed by frost and snow. Should our minds be willing to defy the elements then our bodies often aren't. The dark months are a time to conserve every ounce of energy, for both fish and man. We are more susceptible to sniffles and coughs, and our beds are harder than ever to leave. Sometimes fishing can wait, and given the choice on a cold, dark morning, we pull the duvet back over our heads and drift back to summer dreams.

The widespread apathy to winter angling is one of the reasons I enjoy it so much. I'm not normally unsociable, but there are times when I do not have the energy to share the riverbank with anyone else. It becomes my personal poetical wasteland. A chance to be with my own thoughts, or, more often, to simply be.

Usually, fishermen talk to one another as a matter of course. A fishing rod acts as an invitation to chat and a shared interest breaks down social barriers faster than a bottle of wine. Age, status and purpose are irrelevant as there is always common ground. Yet, while such conviviality should be cherished, sometimes I just want to be on my own.

That said, winter angling is not just about the solitude. Although the fish are less active, they can be more predictable as a result. Feeding spells are likely to be short and affected by water and climatic conditions. Crepuscular light offers safety for prey species to move, while giving predators the chance to stalk unseen; whereas bright sunshine might raise the water temperature that critical degree needed to coax cold-blooded fish into action.

With action sporadic, a winter day on the riverbank develops its own intensity. And, providing I can stay warm and relatively dry, I am perfectly content. Simple pleasures seem to amplify, particularly once the early January blues have lifted and the sun begins to carry a touch of warmth. If a day is cold but dry, my trusty Kelly Kettle flares like a Bunsen burner and a scalding hot cup of tea raises the spirits like nothing else. It is during the period of late winter, as Persephone rises from the Underworld and brings with her the first signs of spring, that as an angler I feel most alive. Primroses and celandines bring yellow warmth to the verges, while in the branches the song thrush clears his throat at dawn and quietens only when the sun has set. Time is precious for a coarse angler. Many of the fish are in their finest fettle, but the season itself is slipping away.

A couple of years ago, my friend Chris Yates and I spent the final few weeks of the season chasing perch in a lake in Wiltshire. Record rainfall had seen the rivers flood like never before and our usual haunts were not just unfishable, they were downright dangerous. It seemed a little odd to be fishing a still water in winter, but the lake itself was chalk-stream fed and crystal clear as a result. We could see every stone on the bottom at eight feet, and so much water was pushing through the lake that there was a steady flow down the main channel.

The extra depth had moved the fish around, too. Pushing them into spots where they might not usually prowl. Chris found some perch skulking around the sunken branches of a fallen willow and we caught a string of good fish up to nearly three pounds. Our final visit of the season coincided with a weather front of high pressure and soft air, the sun quick to burn off the morning mist and leave a soporific spring morning. We knew that the perch were unlikely to feed before dusk, but also knew that they would do then with vigour. We were in the right spot, with the right tactics. It was a simple case of waiting.

The only change to the successful formula of our previous few visits was my rod. On a whim I had borrowed an unused (by Chris at least) and refurbished twelve footer that needed a test run. It was a foot longer than the rod that I had fished with all winter, but that didn't seem an issue as I put it up.

The afternoon passed lazily, with Chris at one point pulling his hat down over his eyes and snoozing in the long grass. As the sun dipped, the perch began to move. I was soon getting bites, though the first few fish were all small. With the sun gone, I hooked something larger, but my rod tip caught in an overhanging branch and the perch shook itself free. I untangled my line and hurriedly recast, but overdid it by an inch and the hook snagged on the fallen willow. I tried to tweak it free but the line snapped and I had to retackle in the half-light. Chris, meanwhile, was catching steadily, each perch bigger than the last, and he teased out a two-pounder just as I was readying to cast again.

In my haste I forgot to breathe and flicked the tackle over the same branch as before. Another inevitable crack followed and I dissolved in a fit of pained laughter. I was in a flap and both the evening and season were nearly over. There was just enough light to tackle up once more, but before I cast Chris urged me into his swim. He had just caught a perch a couple of ounces short of three pounds and was perfectly happy with his lot. Moreover, his swim was more open and I could cast into it with little fear of getting it wrong. There was just one stray willow branch that might be an issue: of course, I flicked the line straight over it. Another hook was left embedded in wood and it was time to lick my wounds and make my retreat.

I was frustrated, but found the episode quite funny. Although I had let the situation get to me, I am sure that had I been using my usual eleven-foot rod I would have had far fewer problems. That extra foot and added weight made it feel as though I was wielding a telegraph pole, and amid the panic and intensity I completely lost my feel.

The fishing rod is not simply an angler's tool; it is a part of him. An extension of his arm through which he can actually feel and sense. With time, fingers wear shallow grooves into the handle and the rod fits as perfectly as an old pair of shoes.

With a little care and no small amount of fortune, a rod will last years – possibly even a lifetime. I once broke two, irreparably, in the course of a single afternoon, yet it seems that the longer I have a rod, the less likely it is to become damaged. With age comes greater consideration, but more significantly the longer that a rod is used the less cumbersome it becomes. Rather like a chef dicing an onion in a stainless-steel blur, the angler almost forgets that the rod is even there.

— ◆ —

Despite the snow storm of yesterday we find the journey through Glen More surprisingly compliant. The road is passable and the eagles are where we hope they will be. To spot two golden eagles and two white-tailed eagles before lunch is more than we could have wished for. When we park at the Kinloch Arms in Pennyghael, we find the pub sadly closed, but the kettle is boiling in the little Post Office next door, where Joy is soon pouring us mugs of warmth to wash down our sandwiches.

After lunch, we head on. I know this spot well but have never seen it so dressed. The view north is eerily splendid. The water of Loch Beg is grey and glassy, and while there is less snow here, a thin blanket reaches down to the high tide line. Ben More, Mull's highest peak, looms to the north-west, a great white ghost that dissolves into cloud long before revealing its whole. The air is still. The world quiet. Waiting. The zing of crossbills busy in the pine trees behind us cuts lightly into the silence.

We drive a short way to the village of Pennyghael, where I am hoping that we might be able to slip off to the south and into the valley of the Leidle. A signpost comes into view. 'Carsaig 4', it reads. This is the point where Alice fell through the looking glass – stepping sideways from a perfect world to find a pocketful of magic for herself. The day-trippers to Mull, those on the coaches that chug between the ferry port at Craignure and the holy island of Iona at Mull's south-west tip, would barely give the sign a second glance. To be fair, considering the spectacular view north across Loch Scridain, few people would notice this innocuous little side turn. For those in the know, however, this is a perfect fit. Carsaig is no more than a small scattering of houses between the pine trees and a wide sweep of beach. It is a hamlet guarded by cliffs that tower a thousand feet above the sea and sheltered against all but the warm, south-westerly winds. Few venture here in the height of summer, and it is clear that now, in winter, not even the locals have attempted to venture out.

The snow lies unblemished along the narrow lane that curves up through the trees, and the route is surely impassable without a snow plough. It's a shame, but time was always going to be tight today. Instead, I will have to content myself with a glance upstream from the stone bridge that straddles the Leidle's final throw. Here, a burn that has tumbled and thrust throughout its length submits gently to the sea.

As a boy, I was once told that sea trout run up the Leidle, and that on a high tide they could be caught here beneath the bridge. I was unconvinced at the time and remain so today. Not so much by their potential existence but by the possibility of catching them. A small spinner worked best, I was assured, but so shallow and rocky is this bay that any cast would surely end with a snagged hook and a broken line. Besides, my childhood self saw no real difference between a trout who stayed at home and one who had gone to sea, and I was quite happy catching the fish that swam a mile or so upstream. I left the sea trout to the otters and spent my time in the deep valley above. A valley which, today at least, I shall be forced to recall only through old memories.

— ◆ —

I can't remember the first time I used a fishing rod. I do remember being bamboozled by the knots and the time it took to set one up. And the tangles, of course – there were so many tangles. Although my early efforts with rod and line were supervised by my father, it was some time before I got to grips with the intricacies of shot patterns and plumbing the depth. Far more straightforward was to thread the rings and tie a hook on the end of the line. Simplicity itself, and a method that will always catch fish. We anglers often tend to over-complicate matters, and to place far too much reliance on the manufacturer of a rod or the complexities of a rig, rather than letting our own understanding of our quarry develop. The fewer barriers that an angler places between himself and the water, the quicker his senses will stretch beyond the confines of his body.

When I first learned to drive a car, my father assured me that in time, I would 'feel' where I was on the road. The car would act rather like a glove, with my senses reaching almost through the metal until I could see distances and hazards that were blind to my eyes. He was right, and a similar relationship evolves between a fisherman and the water. With a rod he no longer needs to get his hands wet, but he learns to feel in a different way.

45

A rod bag soon became a staple piece of luggage on family holidays. We would drop baits off piers and rocky ledges to winkle out small wrasse and pollock, or swing out a float whenever my parents moored up the narrowboat at mealtimes. As our destinations moved further north so other opportunities arose. The small burns and lochans of Scotland were not always off limits to young boys without much of a clue. A polite word with the landowner was normally enough to gain access and in these places I could fish simply and unsupervised. Small brown trout were the inevitable and often only targets, and in some streams, such as the Leidle, they were abundant.

I only ever fished the Leidle with a rod, line and single hook. I would root around the garden at the cottage in Carsaig and collect a dozen worms in an old margarine tub before heading down to the stream. I cannot recall the hook size, but it wouldn't have mattered. These trout were rarely fished for and would have nibbled a scrap of worm were it sitting on a huge, size 2 hook and tied to baler twine. The key to catching them, I discovered, lay in learning where to find them.

I felt slightly daunted when I first fished the Leidle. Or perhaps 'confused' is the better word. The water looked fishless. Just a narrow, rocky cascade. I was used to still, coloured ponds where you could always imagine there were fish because you could see nothing to the contrary. In the chalk streams that I knew in Hampshire, the water would be clear but there would be weed for the fish to hide beneath and trout showing themselves every few yards. I could see no fish on the Leidle, but more importantly I saw nowhere that they might be hiding.

I walked carefully up the valley, hugging the water's edge wherever I could. I hoped to find a long, steady glide – anywhere with a bit of depth – but after a couple of hundred yards realised that I would need to look at the water slightly differently. I stopped just above a tight bend, found a tussock of heather on which to lay my rod, and a boulder on which to sit and think.

The Leidle danced her way down the Glen without a care. She wasn't taunting me, but she had a mischievous glint and would dive left into the heather only to pop up fifty yards to the right. As I watched so my mindset began to adjust. I needed to adapt. The fishing here wasn't supposed to be easy or straightforward, but it would be fun. To make the most of it I needed to stop taking it too seriously.

I looked down into the water directly below me. The bend was cut into sheer rock, the water repeatedly folding over on itself as it tried to negotiate the corner. It was far too turbulent to fish and the next few yards were equally fierce. Above the bend, however, was a wide flat slab of bedrock that the stream didn't cut through but slid over. It was shallow but smooth, and as I watched I noticed a slight crease in the current towards the far side. There was a small step in the rock, only an inch or two in depth, but enough to create a short piece of slacker water. If I were a Leidle trout, and this short stretch was my home, then that is where I would lie.

I reached for my rod and baited the hook, flicking the worm across the flow. The first cast was short but the second was perfect and the worm hit bottom just as it met the slacker water. I didn't see the fish, or feel the bite, but saw the line twitch and lifted the rod instinctively.

There it was. Only a couple of ounces but a perfect little brown trout. Red spots on silver flanks with deep bronze along the back. It was cold to touch; despite the sunshine, the water here was not hanging around in one spot long enough to be warmed. But the trout seemed perfect for it. Cool and sparkling in the summer sun. I slipped it back into the water and it zipped off across the current. I smiled and began to work my way downstream.

It was as if I had opened my eyes to a completely different world. The rushing stream was no longer a teasing tumult but a flood of opportunity. Wherever the current creased or slowed, wherever a rock provided so much as the smallest shelter, a trout seemed to be lying. Before long I was leaving the spots where I felt only the really small fish would be sitting and trying to find something more substantial.

I passed the spot where I had first begun and pushed on with even greater enthusiasm. I found another couple of two-ouncers before the stream dropped into a deep ravine and the terrain forced me away from the water's edge. I had to skirt round a thick, overgrown outcrop before scrambling down a steep slope where the loose earth forced me to slide down the final few yards on my backside.

Here, I found a short forty-yard run before the stream again dropped over a step in the landscape. On this occasion, the drop was sheer and below was a pool that was deep and dark. I worked myself onto the flat rock beside the top of the fall and lowered a worm into the water fifteen feet below me.

After half a minute, I felt a now familiar rattle on the line before the rod tip thumped sharply. This was a better fish, and for a moment I worried that I might not be able to winch it up to me. I had wanted one of quarter of a pound but this was a stunning six-ouncer – and he wasn't alone. I caught half a dozen from that pool, all of a similar size, and headed back to the cottage feeling rather proud of myself. They may not have come on a fly, as many anglers find more befitting for a trout, but in that one afternoon I learned more about the potential of running water than I have done since.

It is many years since I last fished the Leidle. I had wanted to see her today, not to reminisce about past captures but to see the valley in the snow. I love every inch of Mull, yet this small offshoot is where I feel I belong. And the more time I spend here the more I discover. There are secrets in the Leidle valley that are too easily missed should I be overly preoccupied with trout.

Mull is renowned as a wildlife paradise. There are otters all around the coast and dolphins, minke whales and basking sharks off shore. Red deer graze the slopes and adders hide beneath the heather. The greatest treat, however, has to be the eagles. Mull is renowned for its population of golden and white-tailed eagles, and although we had seen fine examples of both this morning, I had hoped to show Dan *my* eagles.

There is a particular ridge near the head of the Leidle to which, in a wind with a westerly edge, the local pair of golden eagles head in order to find lift. Air pushes against the exposed rock which, particularly when heated by the sun, forces a thermal of warmth skywards. Many of the local birds make use of it, and the ravens and hooded crows seem to enjoy riding it as a surfer might catch a wave. I have spent hours just sitting and waiting, listening to the cuckoos and chats, and keeping an eye out for anything looming over the ridge.

A break in the weather is the best time for the goldies, and on my visit here last summer, I got to know their habits rather well. The rain would stop, the sun would pierce the clouds, and I would shoot up the hill from the cottage knowing the eagles would be taking to the air. They would spiral up until they were specks and then launch off down the Ross. I have never looked for the eyrie, and have no intention of doing so, but it must be close as the eagles are quite defensive of their ridge. Other golden eagles will be gently escorted off the premises, while feathers can fly should a larger interloper appear.

On one occasion, the male of the pair appeared first and made good height before the larger, moulting female caught the same thermal. I watched her for many minutes, until she had gained sufficient height to head west and out of sight. As I turned back to the ridge another shape loomed. A young white-tailed eagle was straying where he oughtn't, and although she was beyond the reach of my binoculars, the female golden eagle could still see all that was happening here. She streaked from the sky and sent the white-tailed sprawling. There was no sound; she simply rose up once more, hanging her talons, daring the white-tailed to stay. He didn't, but instead headed rapidly down the glen, reminding himself to give that ridge a wide berth in future.

Today, I will leave the Leidle valley unseen, but with my memories freshened. Dan and I will have to make it back through Glen More before the next snow band hits, but it seems that a great day is set to get even better. The pub in which we are staying is hosting a birthday party this evening for an islander who has turned thirty. He plays guitar and ukulele in a band and the other members are joining him with instruments under their arms and a ceilidh in mind.

Folk by candlelight. It's going to be a rather good night.

4

FINDING YOUR FEET

The Mole

I have a peculiar affinity for Leatherhead. I had never ventured into the town itself until around a decade ago, when a driving job took me off the M25 at Junction 9. I have taken the same route today, joining the orbital a junction to the west. Without a van full of shutters to deliver, I can enjoy a more leisurely trundle through the town, and, in the light weekend traffic, am able to slow almost to a halt as I cross the river on Waterway Road. A couple of hundred yards upstream is the old town bridge and, although I cannot see them all, there are fourteen arches spanning the River Mole. The water itself is a struggle to ignore, but I resist as best I can. The Mole is the reason I am here, and the reason why I have a loose attachment to Leatherhead, but I want to wait another fifteen minutes or so until I look at her properly

once more. I want to see her from the same place that my
teenage self once did.

I was disappointed at first to learn that the River Mole
did not take its name from the mammal. It seemed to fit:
the mole is an animal unseen; we know he is there – and
he certainly leaves enough clues to his presence – but
we don't often see him. When a mole does find himself
above ground, he looks as lost as a fish out of water.
Rather like Mole in Kenneth Grahame's *The Wind in the
Willows*, who was happiest in the sanctuary of his home
and slightly overwhelmed when he first encountered a
river: *'All was a-shake and a-shiver—glints and gleams and
sparkles, rustle and swirl, chatter and bubble. The Mole
was bewitched, entranced, fascinated.'*

Beneath the ground, the mole is a busy burrower. His
front feet are wide – more like shovels with sharp claws,
the perfect tools for excavation. His velvet skin lets him
slide through his tunnels while his whiskers are sensitive
enough to pick up the movement of an earthworm from
great distance. His hills, the bane of the gardener, are
rather useful to anglers. The soil is fine and packed with
amino acids, which are an excellent attractant for fish.
Small balls can be fed into the river to draw attention
from downstream, but as this has no actual food content
a baited hook dangled over the top will be taken instead.

Despite their vulnerability above ground, moles
are surprisingly aggressive. I once 'saved' one that was
wandering across the road and was bitten so hard that

I had to call time on a Frisbee game in order to mop up the blood. Their saliva is mildly toxic and, though I was unaffected, any worm given a nip will be paralysed and then stored in a larder for later consumption.

Perhaps I should remember the mole as Grahame described him: a shy, good-natured creature, well-mannered if a little reticent. And it is his propensity for subterranean living that led to the widespread misconception that this river is so named because it shares his habits. For the Mole is a river that disappears underground.

— 🐟 —

The spot I want to revisit today lies just below Mickleham, a village that retains a sense of seclusion thanks to the A24, which whisks all non-through traffic around the village fringes. I have come further south as I had originally intended to venture up onto Box Hill to try to pick out the path of the Mole as it works its way down towards Dorking. Instead, I pull into a lay-by off the main road where I am reconsidering my plans.

Although it is the weekend and, as I'd hoped, the traffic is lighter, I hadn't considered the cyclists. Box Hill has been a popular destination for cyclists for well over a century. The zigzag road that rises from the west makes for a steep and testing climb, with glorious views at the top. In 2012, the popularity of the route exploded when the cream of the world's athletes tackled it as part of the Olympic road races. It is estimated that over a million spectators lined the course and today it seems like the bulk of them have returned on bicycles of their own. I do not envy them – in fact, as an angler, I normally have little interest in going uphill as I only end up further from the water. But my concern is that I might prove a danger to them. Negotiating cyclists on a road I don't know, with half an eye on the world around me, seems a daft thing to do when it isn't really necessary. So, I decide to leave the pedallers in peace and sit here considering swallow holes.

The lay-by into which I've pulled over is situated in the Mole Gap, a point in the North Downs where clay meets chalk and the river has carved a wide path as it travels north. This is a place of geological peculiarities, with towering river cliffs and a water table that drops well below the level of the riverbed. While the Mole does its best to remain in sight, a series of cracks in the chalk, known as swallow holes, steals away the flow.

There are at least twenty swallow holes dotted along the next mile of river, and between them they reduce the average flow of the Mole by more than 12 per cent. In normal river conditions, this loss of water is barely discernible, but in a time of drought, when the level of saturation within the rock substrate becomes lower upstream, the swallow holes still take their share.

In exceptional circumstances, the Mole runs out of oomph and gives in to the inevitable, slipping beneath the surface. As recently as 2011, the Mole vanished underground between Mickleham and Leatherhead, while the drought of 1976 saw it disappear completely for weeks on end. This is no new phenomenon, however, and possibly occurs less frequently now than in centuries past. On his 1611 map of Surrey, cartographer John Speed left a broken line between Dorking and Leatherhead, above and below which the river is marked in bold. He wrote alongside it '*The River runneth under*', suggesting that the stretch was best known at this point for its subterranean tendency.

Many authors and poets have been inspired by this spectacle. Edmund Spenser, in his 1590 epic poem *The Faerie Queene*, wrote: 'And Mole, that like a nousling mole doth make/ His way still under ground till Thamis he overtake', while in later years the likes of John Milton and Robert Bloomfield were similarly inspired.

Given this distinction, it appears reasonable to assume that the River Mole should take its name from the creature with which it shares a habit. That is certainly the local belief held by my mother, who grew up nearby. However, the name Mole is popularly sourced from Molesey, the town at its end where it meets the Thames. *Muleseg*, as Molesey was originally named, literally mean's Mule's island – with Mule presumed to be the founder of the settlement.

Another theory is that the name is derived from the Latin *mola* – 'mill' – as there were at least twenty mills on the river at the time of the Domesday Book of 1086. This seems less likely, for there were plenty of *mola* on rivers across the country and yet there are no other rivers named

Mole. Names such as 'Avon' (*abona* – meaning river) and 'Stour' ('*sturr*' – meaning strong) can be traced back to Celtic terms. While this creates a rather neat tautology in the case of the River Avon, what is significant is that there are many lesser Avons and Stours meandering across Britain – while the Mole is unique.

After a quick scoot back up the A24, I find myself in another lay-by. This one is really just the well-worn edge of a path that runs parallel with the road. It is the selfsame spot, though, where my mother dropped me off nearly thirty years ago. Back then, I was a fourteen-year-old river-fishing novice, and knew my experience of mountain streams and tickled bullheads would not be much use here. I had been learning my art on ponds and canals, where the wind might occasionally drag my float out of position, but there was never a serious current to contend with. I was nervous but also excited. This was proper grown-up fishing for proper grown-up fish, and there was every chance that there would be proper grown-ups casting a scornful glance in my direction.

It would have been late summer or early autumn when I came here that first time. I certainly remember a thicker barrier blocking out the roar of the road. Today, the yellow of early spring celandines speckle the verge but the only hint of green on the trees comes from the ivy that hugs every trunk. I can see the water from where I stand, but avert my gaze until I reach the arched bridge, where I stand and consider why my first proper river-fishing trip took place on a stream so far from home.

I was twelve when I first joined an angling club. Leigh Hyldon and I had spent weeks distracting ourselves from schoolwork with plans for the opening day of the fishing season. We intended to fish Alresford Pond, a large but heavily silted piece of water on the outskirts of town. I had fished it once before, with my father and brother, and although I had been too young at the time to fully appreciate the experience, I had been struck by the sight of carp cutting their dorsals across the surface far off in the middle of the pond. The school bus took me past the lake twice daily, and I would always try to seat myself on the corresponding side of the coach. Occasionally, I would catch a glimpse of a swirl or ripple that could only have been created by fish, and this stoked my desire to fish the lake once more. When I learned from Leigh that we could join the local angling club as juniors, plans were rapidly hatched.

We left few details unexplored as 16 June approached, marking the start of the new season. We had worked out bait options, tested every float in a dustbin full of water, and been ticked off more than once for neglecting to write up our chemistry experiment results in favour of drawing diagrams of ponds with lily pads, within which we might find fish.

The only stumbling block was the Secretary of Alresford Angling Club – and the fact that we had to visit his house in order to get on the books. His reputation was fierce. We'd heard that, in the past, would-be members had been turned away because they'd knocked on the door too loudly. Those who made it into the house were carefully vetted and, should they answer out of turn, ejected with the secretary's dog nipping at their heels, or, in extreme cases, the barrel of a shotgun pointing at their backside.

Leigh and I were so troubled by the rumours that by lunchtime on Opening Day we were still kicking our heels at the side of Jacklyns Lane. Beside us lay the driveway that led to the Club Secretary's house, but it might as well have been a dentist's doorway for all the enthusiasm we had to approach it. We had learned that the Secretary was particularly surly in the morning, but now we were anxious not to disturb his lunch. The day was drifting while we did little besides flick at stones and let our imaginations get the better of us.

Of course, when we did finally knock, we were greeted by the smiling face of Mrs Club Secretary and offered tea and biscuits while we sorted out our subs. The Club Secretary himself had the vague look of someone who might aggressively wield a pitchfork, but he was doing well to hide it. He was hard of hearing, and fairly officious, but he just wanted to talk about fishing.

When we finally got down to the bankside with our permits that afternoon, we caught nothing. As I think back, it seems interesting that I can recall so little of the actual ticket that allowed me to fish. Perhaps this is because all I got for my £4 was a simple piece of card. There was no great detail on it, no mention of the waters I had access to (all it covered was a single bank of Alresford Pond) and nothing to make me feel as though I belonged to the club.

A year or two later I became a member of a second angling club, and this time the membership card came with bells and whistles. It was even laminated. Unlike the flimsy little card that let me fish at Alresford Pond, the chunky green booklet that came courtesy of Leatherhead and District Angling Society was well worth hanging on to. It was well read – except for the rules section – and even though the opportunity to actually fish seemed dependent upon an alignment of planets, there was always a chance. The newly elected chairman of Leatherhead and District Angling Club also just happened to be an old school friend of my grandfather, which is why I was made a member – to mark the occasion.

Today, as I stand on the arched bridge, an unfamiliar yet distinct bird call draws my attention away from the river. Three ring-necked parakeets squawk their way overhead. A flash of tropical green against a pale blue sky. They were not here when I last visited – though their remarkable colonisation was well underway. As I stand here, their presence stirs a mix of emotions. Some people call for a cull of these birds, fearful of the impact they have on native species. Others argue that they have simply found a niche in the ecosystem, exploiting the food we leave on tables or hanging in plastic. Whatever the attitude taken towards them, they are surely here to stay, and number in the tens of thousand across the south-east – but they are still a novel sight for me. The call is slightly abrasive, like the irritating squeak from a dog's toy, yet they do look splendid in the softest of sunshine.

The water here looks less impressive. After a fortnight without significant rainfall the clouds burst on Friday and have stirred the Mole into a chocolate soup. It isn't pushing particularly high, but is running fast and I wouldn't fancy catching a fish today even if it weren't for the fact that the Close Season already prevents me. A sudden flush of cold, heavily coloured water will send many fish into languor. In these conditions, a stretch that is jumping with fish on one day can seem devoid of life the next, and, during the winter, there is the added impact of snow melt or the salt-laden run-off from the roads. While in spring or summer a rainstorm can taint the river with pesticides and fungicides from nearby fields.

Fish are sensitive to any change in their environment. Being cold-blooded, a sharp change in temperature will immediately impact upon a fish's metabolism. Should the water rapidly cool then the fish become sluggish and lethargic, their heart rates drop and the compulsion to feed disappears. Sight feeders – particularly predatory fish – will show a similar reaction to coloured water: it is a risky business to expend energy unnecessarily when your principal weapon, your vision, is compromised. Hunting blind is a futile venture, and also leaves fish such as these vulnerable to attack from creatures whose senses are better suited to the conditions. Conversely, some prey species will take advantage of such conditions and feed hard in relative safety. Were I to cast today, though, I would be surprised to catch anything more than a minnow.

The bank below the bridge is well worn. This is clearly a popular spot for anglers – not necessarily because it produces lots of fish, but owing to the fact that it is a short walk from the car. Some anglers can be lazy, whereas others might not have sufficient mobility to move far. Then there are those who don't really know what they are doing. As I didn't when I first came here.

My young self plonked his gear on the first piece of flat ground that he found. It is fair to say that I was carrying a lot of tackle that I wouldn't need, but the reason I was so well laden was also why I didn't venture further. This was a completely new experience for me. I didn't have a clue what was going to happen or how I might react. I felt daunted. Although I had read everything I could about river fishing and been so excited in the preceding days that I'd barely slept, the here-and-now was almost overwhelming.

I spent the first few minutes pondering. I was tempted to set up a ledger rod, a simple set-up with a big weight to anchor the bait to the bottom. I could watch the tip of the rod and wait for it to tweak round if a fish took the bait. It would be straightforward but not particularly adventurous, and the books I'd read suggested it was best to search out as much of the river as possible and that was best done with a float.

As I crossed the arched bridge upon which I now stand, I had spotted an angler fishing fifty yards or so upstream. He was trotting the swim – using the flow of the water to carry a float downstream. Small lead shot would be placed down the line in order to sink it and take the baited hook close to the bottom where the fish were most likely to be. As I watched, his float shot under and he lifted the rod tip. He had a fish! It wasn't large but it twisted and flashed on the surface as he reeled it in. I couldn't hide my excitement.

'What is it?' I called.

'A dace,' he answered, before glancing up and offering a smile. 'There're loads of dace in here.'

I'd never caught a dace before. They are relatively small – a dace weighing a pound is considered an absolute monster, and very rarely found away from flowing water. I fancied catching one and, as I considered my options, the tactics of the angler upstream seemed the best to follow. I put up a rod and attached a float, shot and hook to the line. Then I set about plumbing the depth. When fishing a lake or pond it is always important to do this: by attaching a weight on the end of the line that is too heavy for the float, you can work out the exact depth of the water and fish accordingly. In still water this exercise is straightforward, but in the flow of the Mole it was a different proposition. These days, I tend to guess the depth and move the float up and down until I find fish or snag on the bottom, but my younger self spent an age doing battle with the current when it probably wasn't necessary.

In the end, as my frustrations grew, I turned my attention to an area of slack water to my left, and felt a rush of calm as my float finally sat untroubled. It wasn't still for long, however, and although I missed the first couple of dips, I hit the third and lifted the rod to find the smallest fish I'd ever caught on the end of the line. It was a minnow and he was part of a hungry shoal.

Minnows are the bane of many a river angler's life. They are tiny, weighing just a few drams, and voracious – whittling a bait from a hook like a swarm of piranhas. They suffer for their size and are predated by other fish, as well as birds such as kingfishers and herons, and even insects such as water boatmen and dragonfly nymphs. To survive near the bottom of the food chain, minnows live in large shoals, though the benefit of safety in numbers is countered by an eternal battle amongst them for food. Minnows cannot afford to be polite, or overly wary. The smallest scrap of food has to be grabbed before the rest of the shoal get a chance.

That afternoon, I must have caught twenty minnows before the novelty began to wane. I wanted a bit of variety and to catch something a little more substantial. I wouldn't try the main flow as before, though. Instead, I opted to fish the crease between the slack and fast water, and in doing so stumbled upon the prime spot in the swim. A crease in the current is a perfect spot for a fish to lie. Here, it can conserve energy but watch as a conveyor belt of potential food zips past its nose.

I put in a small handful of maggots to stir up the fish and let the float run downstream. After three or four yards it shot under and I had my first ever dace. The fish was only six inches long, but twisted into the main current where it felt twice that size. When I freed it from the hook, it felt wiry in my hand, and was longer and sleeker than the roach that I was familiar with from my local ponds. It was bigger-mouthed, with fins blushed with pink. It looked less dainty than a roach: a fish built for fast currents rather than quiet glides. I caught another, and after another handful of bait, a third.

I began to find a rhythm: feed some maggots, run the float through after them and strike as it dipped. Before long I was catching a fish every other trot, and although a few of the bolder minnows had pushed out from the margins, I also started to catch gudgeon, which I knew from fishing canals, and some roach. Nothing was large, but I was having a lot of fun, although the river was quick to deliver a dose of reality. As I brought another small fish upstream the rod suddenly lurched over and I lost my grip. It had to be a pike, attracted by the activity and grabbing my fish as

I drew it past. My heart thumped and for a moment my mind swam, but I managed to grab the butt of the rod just before it disappeared into the water. With no leverage from a bent rod, there was a crack as the line snapped below the rod tip, and the pike vanished with my fish and all my tackle. The mood of the river shifted. The water seemed to move differently, and the intimacy that had gradually built now crumbled around me quicker than Cheshire cheese.

I grabbed a different rod from my bag and set up a ledger rig. A chunk of lead, heavy enough to hold in place against the current, stopped about twelve inches above the hook. I wanted to catch fish again, quickly, and this would be the swiftest way to get a bait back into the hotspot. I should have waited though; my first cast found a sunken branch and another loud crack left my line lying limp from the rod tip.

I went for a short walk upstream to where the other angler was still fishing. He was cheery and quick to ask how I was getting on. I told him of my successes and then of the pike attack. He didn't seem remotely surprised. As we spoke, he continued to fish, and did so effortlessly. His control of the float was incredible. He moved the rod and steered it along the exact same line again and again, and each time it reached a certain point, it shot under and he brought in another fish. His movements were fluid, and as I watched him my confidence stirred once more.

My dark mood had lifted when I returned to my own swim. I reached for the float rod and set it up carefully, bulking the shot near the hook as the other angler had done. I worked the swim with more vigour, keeping the line off the water as much as I could. The float began to move differently. It seemed to be finding its own way through the swim, riding the crease perfectly. It dipped and then slid under and this time the rod bent hard. I'd caught a chub. My first. The fish wasn't big, only a pound or so, but had brassy flanks that shimmered in the broken sunshine and a dark edge to its fins and tail. I have caught thousands of chub since, many times larger, but that first fish gave me more satisfaction than any other. It made me a river angler.

— ◆ —

I probably wouldn't fish the same swim today. Instead, I would head further downstream where the alders begin to close in and the Mole curves a more mysterious path. I would look to where the undergrowth was thick and untrodden, where I could meld in unseen and withdraw with just a couple of bent reed stems betraying my presence. Below me today, the first few nettle leaves are creeping onto the edges of bare earth. They are sharp and as rich in green as the wings of a parakeet. Beside them the Mole runs dark brown, and although the crease I once fished has been nudged into the bank by the extra weight of water, downstream the surface smooths like the skin of a burrowing animal.

I am glad to have come back, to have relived a pivotal day in my fishing life. But I do not feel compelled to stay and explore. I am aware that my car is vulnerable parked where it is at the roadside, but the state of the river is the main deterrent. The colour of the water leaves me with little to look at or engage with.

And, as I stand here, I sense that while my journey has been filled with positivity and unhindered progress until this point, I am likely to encounter darker times as I head further downstream.

5

BARRIERS

The Avon

I lose a lot of hours standing on bridges – letting the seconds drift downstream until my purpose is lost to the flow. Roads and railways may offer their own stories of days out and journeys to work, but rivers and streams offer a glimpse into an altogether different world. This is a course not yours to follow, but should you allow it, the movement of water can uncrease a cluttered mind. Just as A.A. Milne's Winnie-the-Pooh discovered in *The House at Pooh Corner*:

> Sometimes, if you stand on the bottom rail of a bridge and lean over to watch the river slipping slowly away beneath you, you will suddenly know everything there is to be known.

It is almost impossible not to peek over a precipice. A child on a bridge always has to look, and when he returns five minutes later he has to look again. Similarly, our fascination with water is born from its very mystery.

The muddied water of the swollen Mole could not contrast more with the mid-spring crispness of the river below me. The sun is warm on my back, and the water of the River Avon glistens like the crystals in freshly fallen snow. This is the Hampshire Avon, as steeped in angling folklore as any stream. This place is home to the sort of fish that tremble knees, and over the years has attracted the best anglers from all over the land. It says something about my naivety as a teenager that after such a short river-fishing apprenticeship I should turn my attention to such a heralded place. That said, for a few years fishing had faded behind a haze of hormones and angst, and by the time the rivers flowed back into view I was old enough not to rely on my parents for a lift. I could reach the Avon in under an hour – so why wouldn't I head there?

This is one of two famous Avons that the county of Wiltshire might rightly call its own. The Bristol Avon, though rising in Gloucestershire, curves its way extensively through Wiltshire, while the Hampshire Avon rises and runs for more than half its length before crossing the border into the county after which it is named. Perhaps this is why many of those who live in the river's upper reaches refer to it as the Salisbury Avon, in honour of the county town through which it flows.

Today, I am a few miles downstream of Salisbury and the river at this point has already been joined by all of its most significant tributaries. The rivers Nadder, Wylye, Ebble and Bourne all meet the Avon in and around Salisbury, and swell a stream into a river. There is little discernible difference in volume and flow between the river beneath my feet and that to the south in the town of Christchurch where it meets the sea. This is one of the biggest and most significant chalk streams in the world, draining the plains of Wiltshire before skirting the heaths of East Dorset and the New Forest. It should be noted that, with more than 75 per cent of the world's chalk streams being found in England, where no river is especially long, there is a relevance to the Avon's size, and as part of such scarce habitat, the significance of its ecology is unquestionable.

Chalk is a soft sedimentary rock, created from an accumulation and compression of the calcite shells of microorganisms. When present near harder, less porous rock, chalk presents a river such as the Mole with the opportunity to sneak underground, but here, where the substrate is dominant, the river attains other qualities. Chalk filters rainwater and then stores it, with excess being delivered back above ground via springs. The amount of water leaving these springs varies little, regardless of the time of year, and as a result the temperature also remains relatively constant.

In these sorts of waterway, the acid typically found in rainwater is neutralised by the alkaline chalk and the resulting water holds little in the way of suspended material – letting a chalk stream run with incredible clarity. Even extensive rainfall will not cloud a river such as the Avon for long. The chalk in the surrounding area is constantly absorbing and cleaning the water, so until that area becomes over-saturated and the level of moisture within the ground rises, the river itself remains unaffected. And in an environment where sunlight can filter deep into mineral-rich water, life thrives.

Beneath me are great swathes of water crowfoot. This is a relative of the celandines that glowed yellow in the verges south of Leatherhead. Both are of the genus *Ranunculus*, which includes the familiar buttercup, although the crowfoot has to work hard for its flowers to taste the sun. With roots clinging to footholds in the gravel riverbed, water crowfoot grows long, slender leaves that the current might lead but never teach to truly dance. Instead, they grow tight and trail ever further, until their tips kiss the surface as softly as a seasoned angler lands his line. Here thrust stiff-stemmed stalks above the surface, allowing the predominantly white flowers to open their petals to the pollinating insects of the dry world.

Beneath the surface, each plant supports a delicate pyramid of life. Within the leaves, the flow of the stream is drastically reduced, allowing the temperature to rise a degree or two. Here, microorganisms flourish, as do the insect larvae and the crustaceans that feed upon them. Water snails dot the green fronds, while beetles work between the stems. This is a larder for the fish, and all species will shadow across the gravel, using the crowfoot as a shield against eyes above the water, and make the most of the feast.

When I first stood upon this bridge I watched shoal after shoal sweep past in time with the trailing crowfoot leaves. Dace, roach, chub and perch were present in number, but today all I can see is a smatter of minnows where the flow is weakest. If I wait I am sure I will see the odd fish, but the numbers are no longer there. The Avon has not been well in recent years. Although the water still appears to be clear, the nitrate and phosphorus levels within it have become erratic. Government research has suggested that the chalk aquifers are unable to filter the high levels of agricultural fertilisers that are working their way through the water catchment area. As a result the nutrient levels attract algal growth, which adds to siltation and stifles the growth of plants such as water crowfoot. To compound this, much of the traditional river valley habitat had been tidied away over the years. The small ditches and side streams where small fish and fry could once find sanctuary as they flexed their fins have gone. The extreme weather of the past decade has caused the usually stable water table to rise to record levels, and without these refuges, everything has been washed away.

A further complication has come from Europe. Forced away from traditional wintering grounds in the Mediterranean, flocks of the cormorant sub-species *Phalacrocorax carbo sinensis* were forced inland in search of food. Although already present in small numbers in Britain, suddenly thousands of cormorants were fishing their way through our winter waterways. A healthy river system would have been able to balance against this threat, but the Avon was in a vulnerable state, and fish such as the roach simply vanished from many stretches.

These are sombre contemplations, though in some ways apt. My own journey had darkened by the time that I found this river – my late teens saw the stalling of not just my angling odyssey, but also my life.

— ⬩🐟⬩ —

I loved reading as a child. I had a thirst for learning: facts, figures, the biggest, the fastest. My world was full of cheetahs and Andean condors, volcanoes and tectonic plates. I was a teacher's dream until my early teens, when after a couple of stumbles I completely lost interest. Nothing unusual or extreme – I did what was needed but was no longer driven to shine. The relative anonymity suited me, especially with the need I felt to hide what happened to me each winter.

From the age of ten or eleven, towards the end of the winter I would open my eyes in the morning but not wake up for a week. Today, the world is better educated in mental illness, but it remains a lonely place – especially for children. I couldn't tell my parents what was wrong because I didn't know. I just felt numb, cold and cocooned. I couldn't get up out of bed, let alone give myself a kick up the arse.

Then there was school, and how to explain my absence and my residual fragility to teachers and classmates. As I reached my late teens, these strange days became more frequent and less seasonal. I began to lose months at a time; no sleep, just dreams within a conscious mind. I'd forget how to dress, or walk a hundred yards in the rain before noticing I was barefooted. And I was ashamed, keeping the worst of it hidden, unable to let anyone in. Even keeping myself out.

Eventually I folded, and found myself pumped full of drugs in a hospital ward. Fifteen-minute checks and the laces taken from my trainers. But at last I slept, and was flooded with love from every direction. I was lucky really: there were people in that place who would never leave. Such as the old Italian guy who had paced a strip of carpet bare, smoking his imaginary cigars and never using the toilet. Or the poor woman diagnosed with schizophrenia, addled with a chemical cocktail, placid for all but one minute of my stay – but the end of that minute would see her restrained by half a dozen nurses while others rushed to tend the orderly she had just stabbed. Then there was a lad a year or two older than me who had his memory rebooted every morning with electricity.

'I don't think we've met ...' he would say each morning.

'We have ...' I would answer.

I had a loving family, and more friends than I could wish for. Visitors came daily, with cards and gifts and books. With a clear mind, I read about fish and fishing, and realised that throughout the years the dark days had been studded with light. Or more specifically, steadied by the flow of water.

A small cloud of flies is dancing on the surface beside the line of reeds to my right. They may be a hatch of grannom, I am guessing. They are small and grey and even a skilled entomologist would struggle to identify them from this distance. They have also attracted attention other than my own. A grey wagtail sends them swirling and moments later there is a splash as something beneath the surface takes an interest. I walk back across the bridge hopeful of a better view. It wasn't a big fish, but it was more substantial than the minnows. The wagtail has another dart and then flicks a wing and shoots back beneath me and downstream – shouting its familiar sharp, two-tone call as it flies. There is no further fishy movement, though, and I train my binoculars on the water beneath the flies to see if I can catch sight of the culprit.

My first visit to the Avon, when I had just begun to drive, was made a little further downstream, on the stretch immediately below the town of Ringwood. I arrived in the town early, grabbed a pint of maggots along with my day ticket and found my way to the riverbank. As with my trip to the Mole, I was overladen with tackle. It was warm and as soon as I peered over the edge of the old railway bridge at the top of the fishery, I realised that not only was I carrying too much – I didn't want to be carrying anything at all.

This was a piece of water quite unlike any I had ever seen. The river was wide and fairly deep, yet between the thick beds of weed I could see every stone on the riverbed. And every fish. A small group of very large chub immediately caught my eye. They were drifting slowly across the flow, away from me and to the shelter of an overhanging willow. They were big fish – really big – as was the pike that was lying in the slack water behind one of the bridge stanchions. It was more than a yard long but didn't look out of place. In fact, there was something in her demeanour that suggested there were pike in this stretch higher than her on the hierarchical scale.

Further back into the main flow flitted a shoal of dace. They numbered in the hundreds and, though not large fish, made for an impressive sight. Every second or two one would flash, flipping sideways in the current so that the sunlight bounced sharply off its silver flanks.

Half an hour or more seemed to pass before I remembered to blink. The busyness in my head had gone. A mind that had flitted for so long between darkness and anxiety had finally emptied. I wasn't numbed – or sedated – but was instead soothed, lost to the river. I didn't need to be fishing, I just needed to be beside water. With my gaze blurring to the pulsing current and the flashing dace. Of course, as soon as I became aware of my state, my mind whirred once more into action and rather than settle and drift I hurried off the bridge with my mountain of tackle and found a spot to cast.

The rest of that day vanished. I didn't diary it and the imprint in my memory is an image of someone who looked uncannily like myself stumbling downstream with all of my fishing gear. Then the memory flickers like a candle at the end of its wick and snuffs into nothing.

Today, my binoculars have found nothing beneath the surface, though the flies still dance. I watch as they move, but my senses shift sideways as my ears pick up a distinctive rattle and churr further along the reed line. A sedge warbler swings gently on a stem, voicing his intentions to anyone who might be interested. His song is a collision of noises – wheezes, tchaks, whistles and chirps. It sounds like a dozen different species indulging in some freestyle jazz, not the territorial assertions of a single bird.

My hearing today seems particularly sharp, tuning in as soon as I arrived and silenced the rattle of the car engine. There was a blackbird in the sycamore above me and a song thrush shouting from a few trees down the road. I listened carefully to a wren, robin, blackcap and chiffchaff before my senses rebalanced, with all of the sounds decoded, and I made my way through the trees to the bridge. Now, each time a new sound breaks, my hearing tunes briefly to it. The grey wagtail, the splash of the fish and a distant dog bark, probably from the farmyard upstream. Any new, or less familiar, sounds, such as the call of the sedge warbler, are given further attention. I rest my eyes and nose, allowing my ears to absorb and translate my surroundings. Then, should the sound be ongoing, it softens as it settles into the general hubbub.

The sedge warbler has found his rhythm now. I can pick him out without the binoculars, the pale line above his eye catching in the sun whenever he turns his head. Listening to him has brought me back into this moment. The day is warm but the breeze cool and light, following the river down from the north as it has for much of this spring. The year has slowed in reaction to the cold air. Many of the migrant birds, butterflies and moths are still mooching around on the continent, pondering the value of pushing on. The very fact that I can stand here without puffy eyes and a wad of tissues in my pocket is proof enough that the pollen count is unusually low, although whenever the breeze drops, every plant and flower sends a scent skywards.

I was walking on the beach a few days ago when I got thumped by the most delicious floral waft. After a lull, a puff of wind picked up the scent and thwacked me on the nose with it. I searched for the source among the flowering plants in the pebbles at the top of the beach, but couldn't find it. But what a smell! – my nose, for a moment, was buried in a pot of honey, and I had to close my eyes and hold my breath to take it in. My ears, which had been trained on the scratchy call of a whitethroat, closed instantly with a tinnitus buzz. So intense was that odour that my other senses had to switch off in order to allow my nose to cope.

Here, if I lean as far as I dare over the edge of the bridge, I can catch a slight scent of the Avon. There is a crisp note in the air but in truth the 'smell' is more a cooling of my nostrils than a discernible fragrance. And in late spring, the smell of the river is always submerged in the sea of green that rises up around it. The scent of the nettles is particularly strong at the moment. It isn't especially unpleasant, but can sometimes become overpowering and scratch at your throat as though you are chewing a mouthful of leaves.

I close my eyes and slowly draw a lungful of air through my nose, trying to shut out the nettles and muddy-edged reeds and instead catch a hint of something else. The smells I associate with the early season, such as elder-flower and meadowsweet, are still weeks away. Despite my occasional casts with a fly, I do not spend much time on the riverside in May, but the northerly breeze is not allowing me much opportunity to taste anything new.

I look upstream, into the face of the wind. There is a weir pool a mile or so away that I fished with Chris the winter before last. Conditions had seemed good that day, but we didn't have a bite. A river that had glistened with possibility on our arrival seemed glassy and grey when we left.

— ❦ —

The health of the Avon will bounce back, though, even if it requires a helping hand. There is too much history here for it to be lost. A project to re-establish a self-sustaining roach population to the middle reaches of the river is gaining support and momentum by the year, and there are still pockets of fish to be found around Salisbury. There, the city itself is an unlikely guardian, blocking any local agricultural run-off into the water and deterring all but the most intrepid of cormorants.

The roach of Salisbury certainly swim in some of the most appealing urban habitat. Old Sarum, which is just north of the current city of Salisbury (New Sarum), has been a site of major inhabitation for nearly 5,000 years. Long before the Saxons and Romans called it home, Old Sarum was a settlement for Neolithic Man amidst some of the most archaeologically important landscape in the world. The barrows, tumuli and monoliths that dot Salisbury Plain reflect an area that remains significant historically and sociologically. And throughout that history, the Avon has provided lifeblood, not least in linking Old Sarum with the ancient town of Durrington Walls, a site that lies to the north of present-day Amesbury, which some archaeologists suggest was once the largest Neolithic settlement in Europe.

There is a timeless quality to this river. Mankind has made efforts to harness and control the waterway, but the Avon will not be easily persuaded. For years the ditches and dykes that criss-cross the water meadows have been tidied and occasionally filled, only for the river to swell and remind us that these features are there for a reason. Now, the meadows to my west are once again networked with drains – dry and grassed today, but ready to suck up any extra water that may come in winter. The meadows might be grazed by cattle or cut for hay, but not built upon: we humans are finally realising that water cannot be trifled with when looking for cheap development.

I have mixed feelings as I ready myself to leave. This is a river where some of the most renowned anglers – Dick Walker, Chris Yates, F.W.K. Wallis and Terry Lampard to name just four – have fished and felt inspired. Yet I have had a curious relationship with her. My first visits were clouded with illness, and the memories of those days distorted by the darkness that shadowed me for so many years. Then, more recently, I have returned in better health to find the river in malaise.

I need to recover a sense of balance. The Avon has, after all, provided me with some special moments. A winter catch of dace with a dozen roach over a pound. My friend Kieran Topping's first and only chub, weighing over five and a half pounds. And my father's first ever barbel.

That day, I had taken Dad to a stretch below Ringwood. It was autumn, but the river was still waiting for a decent flush of rain. The crowfoot had lost its vibrancy and on the surface, where the flowers had recently shone, the stems lay curled and yellowed, lolling in the current like seaweed after a storm.

I led my father downstream, through the first two meadows and down to a bend where I had found fish before. At this point, the river turned sharply, cutting a deep and narrow channel that was thick with weed and tough to fish. A short gap in the weed was the only spot you could place a bait, but the water was at least ten feet deep, and the current seemed to fold over itself, dragging the bait around in awkward circles.

At the back of the bend the river grew shallow and the weed thinned beneath the shadow of an overhanging tree. Here, immediately below the high bank, was a neat hole the size of a ping-pong table in the gravel, and the fish seemed to rather like it. I threw in a few handfuls of stewed hempseed and some crumbled luncheon meat and worked my way back down the bank to my father. We would have to keep well back from the hotspot to avoid spooking the fish, so I set a rod up and got my father into position some fifteen yards upstream.

Once we were ready, I crept back down for a peak, inching on my belly for the final few feet. Minnows and gudgeon were flitting excitedly across the bottom, and amongst them were two fair-sized bream and a chub. I watched for some minutes, as the fish grew in confidence. The chub was joined by a second and then a third. It was fascinating to watch them – the oils from the hempseed had clearly stirred their interest but the chub were struggling to find the small grains in among the gravel. A chub's mouth is large, with thick, rubbery lips, suited to the fish's wide-ranging diet. However, it acts as a hindrance when picking up small particles, unlike that of the next fish that swam into view.

A barbel is designed for life on the bed of fast-flowing rivers. His body is shaped like a flat-bottomed torpedo, with low, scallop-shaped pectoral fins. He has four barbules (after which he is named) around an underslung mouth. The barbel is actually heavier than the water that surrounds him, which, along with his shape, allows him to stick to the bottom with little effort. When hooked, he tries to use the current to his advantage, and pulls as hard as any fish, often to the point of exhaustion. It's not unusual, after a particularly fraught fight, for both fish and captor to need a lie-down in the shallows in order to recover.

I put a large lump of luncheon meat onto the hook, big enough to sustain a lengthy whittling from the minnows, and pointed to the spot where my father needed to cast. Then we waited. I had expected a bite to be fairly quick in coming but the moments became minutes and when the rod tip eventually tweaked round we had almost forgotten our purpose in coming there. The fish was on, though, and my father remained calm as he let the rod absorb the barbel's initial charges.

I had yet to catch an Avon barbel and my heart was thumping as though I was the one playing the fish. But

Dad is always measured at such moments and played the fish as though it was his hundredth barbel, not his first. It was a stunning fish, with scales the colour of butter edged in bronze, and fins blushed with scarlet. We didn't weigh it, though it looked to be a few ounces over five pounds, and rested it in the gentle current below the bend before watching it power off back into the main flow.

I smile as I recall the moment, and the waters of the Avon below seem to clear once more. I am dogged by depression to this day, even if the clouds never crowd as densely as they once did twenty years ago.

I will be back soon to fish the Avon, maybe next winter when those Salisbury roach will be in their prime. In the meantime, I let my thoughts drift downstream and ponder the words of Friedrich Nietzsche ...

No one can construct for you the bridge upon which precisely you must cross the stream of life, no one but you yourself alone.

6

TRIBUTARIES

The Itchen

A lot can happen in four years, and yet at the same time nothing seems to change. Winchester Station is very different, with a new, roofed footbridge, glass-walled with garish orange banisters lining the stairway. There is further change at the junction outside. New buildings, a new supermarket, and one exit seems to have vanished altogether. The Albion is still there, thank goodness. It was always a welcome place to have a crafty pint before catching a train.

I make a brisk zigzag through a couple of back streets, past the King Alfred, another old watering hole, and all of a sudden everything is back where it should be. There are the flutey notes of a blackcap, the short shrill alarm call of a moorhen and the sight of an old friend – just as I remember her.

The Itchen is a river that has meandered through most of my life. I was born within a mile or two of her, and for many years lived within walking distance of the river herself or one of her tributaries. Now, having cut my ties with her and moved west, I wonder if I really made the most of her.

Hampshire may not have a unique claim to the Avon, but it can count two of the most famous trout streams in the world as its own. Both the Test and the Itchen flow wholly within the borders of the county, and both are visited by anglers from around the globe. Here flows water within which no amount of money might buy the right to fish. Stretches where only the nobility may tread and where the 'Private Fishing' signs stand like portents of doom. In fact, they were likely hammered into the gravel with the limbs of vanished poachers of the past.

The Itchen was very much off limits to me as a child. There wasn't a bridge or path that passed within fifty yards of the river that wasn't decorated with one of those threatening signs warning me to keep away. I would enjoy walks beside the river, glimpsing the trout and pike within, but had to content myself with fishing on the local ponds.

I didn't have a serious crack at the Itchen until my mid-teens, when I ventured into Winchester with a school friend, Graeme Lawes, in order to try our luck on a free stretch in the city. It was tough going, and after a few hours we had almost run out of bait and had still not had a bite. In desperation, I tore the corner off my sandwich and stuck it on the hook, floating it downstream and following it down the bank. After eighty yards or so there was a swirl and the line tightened. I'd caught a brown trout of two pounds twelve ounces and saved an otherwise dour day.

That catch took place further downstream from where I now sit; the water beside me here is actually a side stream that has slid off the main river for a short half-mile adventure of its own. I am resting in the shade of a huge sycamore, sitting loosely upon a knot in its trunk. The air is cool and the grass thick and damp. The sky is almost cloudless, but not even the slightest dapple of sunlight is making it through the canopy. The stream slows at this point, almost as if the tree were sucking up so much water that it has halted the flow. I often used to find a pike lying here, in the gap between the weed beds; in fact, one was in residence when I arrived a few minutes ago, but I was walking too clumsily and it vanished in a cloud of silt. Since I have been sitting here, though, a perch has drifted into the pike's lie. It's a good fish too, at least a pound and a half – possibly more. It sits perfectly still, just a slight movement of its mouth and gills as it filters oxygen from the water.

The perch is a handsome fish: short and stocky, with a deep-green back which fades into yellow and then white under the belly. It wears a series of thick stripes down its flanks, normally five or six, with the one below the back of its dorsal fin split in two. Ah yes – the dorsal. Sharply-spined, it concertinas like a geisha's fan. The foremost spine stands proud of the webbing and is a handy deterrent to any passing pike or otter. The perch's fins are bright red, and all of its colours appear more vibrant in clear water, as is the case for the fish I am watching. A perfect, bristling specimen.

I had hoped to see a perch or two here. They are species that only started appearing in this part of the river around fifteen years ago. Or, at least, that was when I first noticed them. The perch population crashed in the 1960s and 70s: this once numerous fish all but vanished as 'perch disease' spread across mainland Britain from an initial outbreak in south-east England. The exact cause of the outbreak was never determined, and modern efforts to discover the source, and hopefully prevent a repeat, have been inconclusive. It is, therefore, a reasonable assumption that a river such as the Itchen should have lost its perch altogether.

Prior to the outbreak of the disease, the perch would still have had a hard time of it. Any fish in the river would have had to evade the attentions of professional river keepers tasked with removing any non-game fish. Such was the money that people would pay to cast for salmon and trout, that all other species were deemed a nuisance – an attitude that was an unfortunate hangover from the nineteenth century.

Victorian culture saw a huge surge of interest in the Great Outdoors. The expansion of the railways had opened up access to the countryside like never before, and city dwellers had a new playground to exploit. As interest in field sports grew, with it came an increase in the persecution of hook and claw. This was nothing new – humankind has ever endured a tempestuous relationship with other apex predators. In Britain, animals such as the wolf and lynx existed in direct competition at the top of the food chain, and were driven to extinction as a result. Smallholders and farmers lived on a knife edge, and a single lamb taken by a fox or white-tailed eagle could have a devastating impact on a young, crofting family. Unfortunately, this wholly understandable need to preserve life and livelihood became diluted by Victorian fanaticism. Protection spiralled into species genocide and unfounded hatred. The white-tailed eagles went the way of the wolf, lynx and bear. Otters and pine martens were driven to the brink. On many rivers, pike and perch were classed as vermin, and systematically removed.

In nineteenth-century Britain, mankind's influence upon the natural world was becoming ever more marked – and yet we remained blind to the consequences as we were too busy playing God. Should humans really have any right to decide what species should live or die? It seems horribly arrogant to place ourselves in such a position. To dress ourselves up in such power and authority. To consider ourselves so superior to any other living thing.

Fortunately, modern education has led to greater toleration and appreciation. A twenty-first-century gamekeeper is far more likely to stand and admire a red kite than feel an urge to shoot it. In fact, were it not for the existence of shooting estates then our countryside would face further decimation. The hawthorns and cover crops planted to protect pheasants and partridges also provide shelter and food for our traditional farmland species. Were there no shooting, and no gamebirds, then this vital habitat would disappear with the remaining hedgerows. Ploughed into the ground and replaced by an arable desert.

— ❦ —

The Itchen valley has certainly benefited from the esteem within which its fishing is held. It is not a particularly long river – twenty-eight miles from source to sea – but from the moment it bubbles up from the aquifer beneath the village of Cheriton it seems to draw life to it. For a few miles, it flows north until it meets the River Arle and the Candover Stream just to the west of Alresford. The Candover used to flow freely through the valley in which I grew up, but has, sadly, become ever more of a winter bourn in recent years. Excess extraction has seen the water table drop and during the summer the stream no longer flows through the villages which take its name.

Yet one of our most threatened species is clinging on between the Candover's narrowing banks. The white-clawed crayfish was once widespread, requiring clean water – although not necessarily much of it. An expansive diet allows them to be fairly adaptable, but due to their secretive, nocturnal movements, they often go unnoticed. They look a lot like small lobsters and wield

94

fearsome-looking claws, but they are naturally timid, tucking themselves safely out of sight of otters and herons.

Sadly, the fortunes of the white-clawed crayfish changed with the introduction, in the mid to late twentieth century, of their North American cousin, the signal cray. The signals were imported largely as a food source, but were stocked extensively without restriction and spread rapidly, carrying with them a plague that has almost wiped out the native white-claws. Their impact upon the entire ecology of many of our rivers and streams has been immense. In recent years, the signal population has exploded, eating fish eggs and invertebrates, clearing weed and loosening banks. They burrow into substrates, colouring the clear streams and lowering oxygen levels in the water. On some smaller watercourses, there is practically no life left other than the signal crayfish, who then cannibalise each other in order to survive. In time, they may find a niche in the ecosystem, but for the moment their presence is devastating and could well lead to the extinction of the white-claw.

When I was young, peering over the railings into the shallow water of the Candover Stream, I had no idea that such an apparently insignificant piece of water might one day play such an important role in protecting one of our native species. Yet I know the signals are coming. The isolation of the Candover will keep it safe for a time, but rather like the fate that met the alien invasion in H.G. Wells' *The War of The Worlds*, we could do with a crayfish version of the common cold to snuff out the colonists.

— ◄═ —

The perch is still there. Dorsal fin erect – watching and waiting.

I feel the urge to leave the shadows now. As my heart rate has slowed, my skin has cooled and prickles as if to urge me back into the sun. My thoughts drift away from the perch and the river, and I become aware of the birdsong in the reed beds behind me. Here, the sedge and reed warblers are in good voice, yet I cannot hear the bird I was hoping to find. A slow walk around this little nature reserve might bring some joy, though, and it will very likely lead to the other of my hoped-for sightings.

If I close my eyes, the sound of the breeze in the reeds takes me to the sea. I am reminded of the great beeches at Stourhead, six months earlier. The temperature is similar today, but the warmth is very different. The sun is high and fierce, but the breeze is following the northerly bearing that has typified this spring. Back in the autumn, the warmth came from within the slowly baked earth. A sleepy, slightly heavy air.

Today feels fresh and clean, though were I to kick off my flip-flops, the soil would feel cool as the grass did beneath the shade of that sycamore. Around me, a sea of colour sways with the sun. The deep yellow of the iris is beginning to fade, while a shower of spent hawthorn blossom scatters with every gust. The elder is on the march, fresh crowns seeming to flower as I stand and watch. The hedgerow is thick with them, while beneath is a battle between the white of cow parsley and the pink of the ineptly named red campion. I cannot smell any of them – not from where I stand. The scent of the reed bed dominates. A heavy, stagnated must, which reminds me of early-season visits to old steaming pools. There are plenty of warblers in voice. Reed and sedge, Cetti's, blackcaps, chiffchaffs and whitethroat. But still not, as I had hoped, a grasshopper warbler.

When I lived locally I would regularly walk around this reserve in spring. Winchester is a leafy and affluent city, yet there is still a sufficiently pleasing contrast between the dust and bustle of its streets and the haven of this secret pocket of nature. To the east are industrial estates, dual carriageways and the roar of the M3, but with some filtering of the sound, I could be almost anywhere. At moments in the past, I would step into this place to find sanctuary from myself. Dark days when I wouldn't hear birdsong or see colour on the hedgerows, and would barely notice the water. Coming here was a step sideways; I wasn't going anywhere and had no purpose being here, yet it was all I needed. A chance to get off the ride for a few moments – even if getting back on might be tougher as a result.

It wasn't until that mental fog lifted that I first noticed the treasures among the reeds. And my favourite was the grasshopper warbler. These are secretive birds that skulk between the reed stems and scuttle through low cover like a mouse on a woodland floor. It is their song for which they are named, a long unerring, whirring reel that rises and falls as the bird turns its head. It is a sound that I am beginning to hear less frequently each year, and not just because the species is in steady decline. The mechanical tone rattles at a pitch that older ears cannot hear. When I brought my parents here to listen to the warblers – the grasshopper in particular – my father couldn't pick it up at all. We stood within yards of one reeling bird, yet he heard nothing. Of course, if my mother and I were not there to tell him, he would not have been aware of either its presence or the fact that his ears couldn't register it.

The loss of hearing with age is a curious thing. My friend Chris speaks of sitting with his children when they were young, watching bats at dusk. He told them about the high-pitched noises the bats would be making and was met with quizzical looks. His children could hear the squeaks of the bats very well; it was their father who could not.

We are never fully aware of all the sounds we lose as we grow older, yet we nevertheless persist in presuming that other people share exactly what we hear. I cannot remember hearing bats as a child, but at the time I would not have considered the sounds as anything but normal. I would not have known that I wouldn't hear those sounds as I got older; nor were there any adults there to warn me. After all, they could no longer hear them at all.

— ◂━ —

I find myself beside the main channel of the Itchen, which runs along the eastern edge of the reserve. The river turns at right angles here, and I am on the apex of the bend, with yards of river visible in two different directions. Otters are active throughout the Itchen valley, and are now regularly seen in Winchester itself, but the mammal I hope to see today is somewhat smaller. It doesn't take long – this was always a good spot for sighting one. A water vole. Once common but now in desperate decline. Over 90 per cent of our water voles have disappeared; much like the white-clawed crayfish, this is an animal facing extinction in Britain.

This particular vole is busy. He hugs the left-hand bank, swimming with a steady and endearing doggy paddle. Water voles are full of personality, and, like the kingfisher, a sight that anglers might almost be guilty of taking for granted. Spending so much time beside a river enables the angler to become part of the furniture: species that other people might spend hours searching for will very often arrive at an angler's feet.

He's dived. Spooked by a low-flying woodpigeon. For such a slow, deliberate little mammal, the water vole can certainly shift when he needs to. Not that the woodpigeon presented any sort of threat. Perhaps it is time I moved too. There are a couple of other spots I want to look at before my train leaves.

— 🐟 —

There are historical echoes wherever you walk in Winchester. Originally an Iron Age settlement, the Romans found the spot to their liking and built a vast (for Roman times) walled town they called *Venta Bulgarum*. In medieval times, Winchester became the capital of Wessex; this was where King Alfred masterminded his Viking repulsions but forgot to take the cakes out of the oven.

The cathedral – Europe's longest – dates back to the eleventh century and dominates the cityscape. I catch regular glimpses of it as I work my way downstream, but shall not venture any closer than the river will take me. I pause at the spot where Graeme and I once fished as schoolboys. I've cast here a fair few times since and caught a few fish. Considering my proximity to the city centre, there is a tranquil feeling to this short stretch. Although the riverbanks are reinforced, there is space here for the Itchen to breathe. Behind me, the red-brick terrace sits beyond a wide grassy strip and a dead-end road. The buildings that back onto the opposite bank, one of which used to be the best pub in the world, muffle the urban rattle.

So often rivers are strangled in our cities. Squeezed out by the very life they help create. In London, many streams are 'lost' altogether. Sent underground through sewers and tunnels so that every inch of space above can be exploited. Though extreme wet weather has seen the Itchen slip out of her banks in this part of Winchester during the early part of the twenty-first century, for the most part she slips through without any anger or ferocity. And despite the fact that some of her treasures find themselves snuck home and introduced to lemon and dill, there is a healthy stock of fish in the river as it weaves through the city.

Brown trout, pike and grayling are the mainstay, but as with the perch that I watched an hour or two ago, the coarse fish are steadily increasing. Roach in particular can be found in vast numbers. When living on the outskirts of Winchester, and exploring every inch of side stream and backwater, I saw some very big fish. Yet, as a rule, the roach is not an especially large fish and seeks safety in numbers. As they age, and their shoal mates get picked off by pike and disease, they grow ever more wary. They start to keep to themselves, leading a solitary existence and leaving the harum-scarum life of the main flow to younger and more energetic fish. In fact, these big old roach behave so differently from their smaller selves that they could easily be a different species. Without the competitive nature of shoal life, they can take forever to decide on their dinner, and develop a fickle nature that infuriates the angler.

A little further downstream, where I will walk to if I have time, I spent a couple of seasons chasing a small group of very large roach. They were wonderfully unpredictable. Never lying in the spots where they really should, in the holes or under cover. Instead, they would spread out and sit in open water where they seemed more vulnerable. There too, it was difficult for me to hide myself from them, yet they rarely panicked. They seemed to sense the danger rather than react to my shape, and would drift slowly away, dissolving into the blanket weed or simply disappearing.

I tried every trick to catch one. Using the lightest of lines and tiniest of hooks. Free-lining baits, float fishing and ledgering. I tried early mornings and after dark, but I only twice hooked a roach – and I lost them both. Yet I found the experience fascinating, and spent far more time watching the water than actually fishing. The roach simply couldn't be stirred to feed with any kind of enthusiasm. Occasionally, one or two of the fish would nose around and even pick up the odd piece of bait, but even a stream of maggots, which rarely fails to coax a response, would be met with indifference.

Nevertheless, I caught plenty of other fish as I toiled. Lots of grayling and brown trout, some lovely perch, a few pike and even a bream, which was the only time I have seen one in the area. And all the while the roach would drift lazily through the weed stems like coils of mists twisting through a forest.

— ◆ —

A fish suddenly splashes through my thoughts. It rose a little way downstream and, although I didn't see it, I'm fairly sure it was a moderate-size grayling. While they

102

will feed with abandon in the thick of a mayfly hatch, trout tend to break the surface with a little more caution than grayling. The latter, particularly when small, tend to charge about, and the splash I heard was sharp and short like a wine glass smashing on a solid floor. Were it more of a 'gulp' then I might have suspected a trout, and had there been significant sideways movement then it might have been a pike making a strike at its lunch.

There are few flies in the air today, though the cool breeze will slow any hatch until the early evening lull. The bulk of the mayfly will have already flown, and although there will likely be a cloud or two this evening, they will not billow so densely that the fish lose every inhibition.

On one such evening, when the air was thick with insects, I popped down here after work with a fly rod and found the scene slightly surreal. Every fish in Winchester seemed to have converged into fifty yards of foaming water – hurling themselves skyward, crashing and thrashing. I was so transfixed that I didn't notice the hatch ease, and by the time I had threaded the rings on my rod the waves were reduced to ripples. I rose a couple of fish but was struggling until a far more experienced hand offered counsel. He nosed through my fly box and shook his head – I had nothing bold enough.

'Try this,' he said, offering me an enormous mayfly imitation, as yellow as the sun and very nearly as big. It was taken instantly, and my guide gave me a wink before wandering off to find a fish of his own.

I do wonder if a fly might have been the answer to the roach. Possibly a nymph imitation, on a slow-sinking intermediate line, gently tweaked back across the noses of the fish. The thought is quite tempting, not that I have a rod with me today. But revisiting the Itchen has changed my perspective of the river.

For many years the relationship I shared with my local river differed from any other. I would drive for an hour to fish the Kennet or the Avon, yet never be drawn to cast into the Itchen. As I have walked around Winchester today, I've begun to understand why. I have spent too much time here – or more specifically, my formative self spent too much time here. Some lovely memories have been stirred as I have walked the city, not least by the sight of the wall opposite me, beside which I stole a kiss from the girl who is today my wife.

Also evoked, however, are less pleasant reminders. There are more shadows here than there really ought to be and some of them are truly dark. Often, when the clouds were at their thickest, I would find myself beside the river. I had no interest in fish or fly hatches, water voles or grasshopper warblers. But the movement of water was a comfort. The constant inconsistency. I spent hours simply sitting, once through until dawn, as the river gently numbed me.

In some ways fishing elsewhere completed the escape that I sought, but I also suspect that the Itchen provided a different diversion. I mentioned this to Sue, my wife – not while kissing her beside the wall I should add – and she reminded me of the words of the Turkish playwright Mehmet Murat Ildan:

> Ask the river, where it comes from? You will get no answer. Ask the river, where is it going? You will get no answer, because the river lives inside this very moment; neither in the past nor in the future, in this very moment only!

Although the Itchen exists within a single moment, it still flows with an element of my past. That current is not nearly as strong as it once was, but it is enough for me to leave today satisfied in the knowledge that I will not rush back. I will return one day – with a rod and a sense of adventure – and when I do, I shall be very happy to be here.

7

FINDING IDENTITY

The Kennet

So often it is only when we stop looking that we find exactly what we are looking for. Not just the car keys or that book on butterflies you put down last summer and haven't seen since. But things less tangible, such as love, friendship, and contentment. There is no great mystery to this; it's more a case of allowing one's mind to be receptive. Strive too hard or with too much purpose, and we can distort the values of our goals. We find fault where there is none to find, or paper over cracks that really should be filled. While it is impossible to experience every situation in which we find ourselves with an entirely open mind, with greater dispassion comes greater understanding. If we are agreeable then, I believe, we will find a world filled with greater opportunity.

I wasn't looking to embark upon a harmonious journey when I first came to the River Kennet, nor do I recall any instant, profound connection with the watercourse. Yet the Kennet soon began to flow through my subconscious, much as it still does today. My dreams were not filled with fishes, but the river itself was an intrigue, and my guide, Martin, had plenty of his own captures to relate.

Life was nudging me around when I found myself at Basingstoke Technical College. Failure elsewhere and a decidedly green attitude had left me attempting to follow the paths of others; but this new path led me into the lives of people that I remain eternally grateful to have met. Here was a crowd united by musical taste and a sense of mainstream discord – not outcasts by any stretch, but people happy to skirt the rigours of normality. I hadn't thought I would meet a fellow angler among them, but as it transpired I had much in common with Martin. He too had a love of wildlife, particularly birds, and a sensible appreciation of football. Best of all, though, he had caught barbel, and he was willing to show me where.

More than two decades have passed since I first stood on this bridge with Martin. Today, I am on my own and the sight below me is very different. If the Hampshire Avon is a river in decline, then the Kennet is almost at the bottom of the pile. The beds of water crowfoot that once billowed from bank to bank beneath this bridge have almost gone, and despite the low water level, there is a peculiar, milky tinge to the water. It is hard to believe the contrast. On that first morning, Martin pointed out a barbel within moments. Then another – and another. There were literally dozens of fish drifting between the weed fronds and goodness knows how many more out of sight. The gravel was warm and golden and the bronze-backed barbel quite difficult to discern against it. Once I had my eye in, though, the bottom seemed to be alive. The pectoral fins stood out. They are large, scallop-shaped and pinkish in colour, and easier to pick out than the scale-patterned backs of the fish. There were chub too, and a huge shoal of dace. All swimming in crystal-clear chalk water.

That's not to say that the fishing was easy. Such was the health of the Kennet in those days that the natural food levels offered more than enough sustenance for the fish. I always found plenty to keep my interest, and over time learned how to catch a few of them. On occasion, with good fortune and the right conditions, the catches were spectacular.

Were I to fish this river today, however, I wouldn't fancy my chances.

Boat traffic on the Kennet and Avon Canal is widely blamed for the turbidity in the former. Originally built to aid passage between London and Bristol, by the 1950s the canal had fallen into disrepair. In 1962, the Kennet and Avon Canal Trust was formed with the aim of restoring the canal to full navigable use, and after three decades of work this was achieved. Eighty-seven miles of navigation was now available to boaters, canoeists, walkers, cyclists and, of course, anglers.

The issues for the Kennet today stem from the fact that, downstream from Newbury, the river and canal are quite often one and the same watercourse. With a steady chug of narrowboats, the silt in the canalised stretches is steadily stirred and carries colour into the streamier areas of the river. That this has some effect upon the appearance of the Kennet is beyond argument, but it is far from being the *real* issue. The Kennet, like the Avon, is a chalk stream reliant upon the purifying properties of the chalk aquifers at its source. Yet even above Newbury, where the canal traffic has no influence upon the clarity of the water, the Kennet is not as it should be. The delicate balance of a chalk-stream habitat struggles to cope with the pressures put on it by twenty-first-century demands – and the Kennet is no exception. Every year the population across Britain rises and demand for freshwater increases, placing a strain on our existing reservoirs and water courses. A planned pipeline that will offer alternative water supplies to Swindon would ease the demands placed upon the Kennet, but for now 'The Lady of the South', as she is tra-ditionally known, is gasping.

The ancient Neolithic monuments and archaeo-logical treasures of Wiltshire seem to centre around Swallowhead, where the Kennet bubbles from the ground. Immediately to the south is the West Kennet Long Barrow, a burial chamber more than 300 feet long; while to the north, and dominating the local landscape, sits Silbury Hill. Though not quite a hundred feet high, Silbury Hill is man-made and comparable in size to the pyramids of Egypt. Its purpose has long been debated, but its creation dates back to Neolithic history when the Long Barrow and the Stone Circle at nearby Avebury were also built. With such prominent landmarks in such close proximity to one another, the significance of this area to ancient humanity is difficult to comprehend. Perhaps the source of the Kennet was the key – and the barbel that swim within it the inspiration. When I first encountered them, these fish certainly caught my attention quite unlike any other species has done before or since.

The barbel is a fish of weir pools and swift currents where they move effortlessly – those fish that Martin and I first watched seemed to glide as if suspended in air. Slipping between the crowfoot with barely a flick of tail or fin, using their muscular frame and bulk to hold station with ease.

As I mentioned earlier, barbel are prone to fight to the point of exhaustion and, to the unwary angler, this can cause an issue. The fish often needs time to rest and in extreme cases will need to be supported in shallow water for some minutes before release as it pumps water back through its gills.

I'm aware that taking such care of a creature that only minutes earlier was being actively pursued might seem peculiar. And herein lies one of the oddities of fisherfolk, the vast majority of whom care deeply for the fish that they catch. Angling is a practice that has gone beyond the act of hunting for food. Aspects of it remain in many ways a sport – match fishing is exactly that – but the deeper an angler immerses himself in his occupation, the greater his respect for his quarry and the habitat in which it lives.

Anglers are ever alert to the condition of the waterways in which they fish, and often the first to notice issues of pollution or low oxygen. The life within a river is the simple barometer of its health, and other water users are not so intrinsically linked with this. It is the anglers, and those who represent them, who are making the most noise about the state of the Kennet, for example. Their anxiety and calls for action are then heard by organisations and conservation groups with greater clout and resources – and, as a result, action will hopefully be forthcoming.

The barbel population within the Kennet is very different today from when I first fished the river – and a world away from the numbers that swam here forty or fifty years ago. My friend Peter Arlott, who has lived beside and fished the Kennet for over sixty years, talks of a time when the barbel population was at its peak. In a single evening, he caught a hundred fish between two and four pounds in weight.

Today, you will do well do catch a hundred Kennet barbel in a season; yet with less competition, those fish that do survive have grown in size. This has kept the interest of those anglers driven by the capture of specimen-sized fish – people keen to see their faces in the pages of angling magazines and newspapers – but as the barbel population dwindles so concerns mount.

The issue isn't only about the decline of the barbel, although they are the species with which the Kennet is most associated and without them the river will lose an enormous chunk of its identity. The barbel is indigenous to the Kennet, as they are to the Thames, into which this river flows. Though they are now widespread, historically barbel were found only in easterly-flowing rivers – those that were once linked to the Rhine at a time when Britain was part of mainland Europe. Over time, largely during the twentieth century, barbel have found their way into rivers across England, Wales and even Scotland. Many official stockings have been made, but just as many unofficial fish movements have seen these fish establish themselves in places where they have never previously been found. This spread has been greeted favourably by many anglers. Indeed, it is partly the esteem in which the barbel is held that has led to the expansion of its range. However, some anglers are less pleased, particularly when the fish appear in rivers where salmon and sea trout might breed.

Fish eggs are a prime food source for all manner of fish, mammals and invertebrates – and barbel are no exception. They will eat the protein-rich ova of salmon and will truffle around in pacey areas of water where other fish might not feed so efficiently. The potential impact of barbel upon existent fish stocks is undoubted, yet for the most part, they seem to find a niche. No other fish seems able to adapt so well to life between the swaying crowfoot leaves on swift, gravel runs; and although numbers of barbel may initially boom when they populate a new watercourse, they subsequently settle.

For those concerned with salmon and trout stock, some peace of mind can be found in the fact that barbel require higher water temperatures than those fish do in which to breed. Due to their formation, the upper stretches of chalk streams run at a steady temperature regardless of the time of year, but there the water is not warm enough for barbel to spawn. For nearly twenty miles the Kennet flows too cold for the barbel, with fish very rarely found as far upstream as Kintbury. Instead, the eggs of salmon, sea trout – and barbel – face a different and relatively new threat.

— ⋅●⋅ —

I have stepped down from the bridge, and worked my way downstream a hundred yards or so. The river shallows for a short stretch, and skiffles over the gravel. Here, at least, is a better growth of weed, but it looks tired, the vibrancy of lime green replaced with lank brown.

The bank here is firm beneath my feet and for a few yards is solid and uniform in shape, suggesting it may have been reinforced once. The depth of the river increases sharply here, the water slowing as it does so, and to the left below me is a deep slow eddy. There used to be a willow that curved over the water at this point, forming a cave within which the current slowly turned. Today, though, only fragments of the willow remain – pollarded over time by the wind. A series of smaller trees, hawthorn and an alder, have leapt up in its place and I am struggling to find my feet despite the hours I have spent here in the past.

As a young man, I always liked to fish this swim. It used to be awkward, and despite the changes still looks as though it is; but that was the attraction – it put other anglers off. This is where I took my first float-caught barbel. Casting a bait directly into the cave of branches was impossible without snagging the line, so I worked a float into the eddy and let it drift slowly round. After half a dozen lazy circuits it dragged to the right and I bent into a fish. It was a lovely fight, the barbel diving first for the roots of the willow and then the sanctuary of the weed bed in the main flow. I eased gradually upstream and netted it first time. It weighed eight and three quarter pounds – a really good fish for me at the time.

Float fishing wouldn't be quite so advantageous today; in fact, it would be easier to fish from the opposite bank. And, as I look more closely at the movement of the current, I notice that the eddy itself seems to have fizzled to nothing. It may have been clogged up with fallen branches from the willow, but reeds are encroaching into the margins and I doubt the depth is anything close to the seven or eight feet that I used to fish into. At the water's edge, beside my feet, I can make out the bottom through the fug. Here the water is only around eighteen inches deep and the gravel bottom has been lost to sediment. There are no fry to be seen – in fact, no life at all, save the ominous form of a signal crayfish that moves across the mud like an armoured tank. It is fairly average in size, maybe six inches long, and oozes menace. The Kennet is thick with them. On the River Lambourn, a tributary of the Kennet, a population of white-clawed crayfish remains, but rather like those on the Candover Stream, I suspect their days are numbered.

And it is the signal crayfish that poses the bigger threat than the barbel to salmon and sea trout. They will eat the eggs of all fish, and care little for cooler water temperatures. As they burrow into banks and unsettle the silt and mud, so the river colours with the sediment. It isn't just narrowboats causing a stir.

It is hard to know which way to head. There are miles of river both up- and downstream of where I am standing, which I have fished my way along in the past. In moments of indecision, it is sometimes easiest to go with the flow and, in the end, I'm glad that's what I've decided to do. Here I am, retreading paths that I haven't walked for over fifteen years, and while there is familiarity about them, there is much more that has changed.

There is an oft-quoted phrase from Henry David Thoreau in his summation of *Walden*, an account of the two years, two months and two days he spent living wild in a cabin in the woods: 'Things do not change; we change.' To place his words in context, Thoreau, a leading member of the Transcendentalist Movement of the nineteenth century, was urging his readers to resist the trappings of materialism: a sunrise looks the same whether you are rich or poor; all one must do is look for the simple pleasures and find contentment within oneself. I'm fond of Thoreau and agree with him that we shouldn't feel obliged to react to fashion or social pressure; for example, a well-kept pair of boots will still function if they are two or ten years old – it is only our attitude that sees them differently. Acceptance of ourselves for exactly what we are, is, in Thoreau's mind, the key to happiness. And of course he is right; it is a sentiment that seems particularly relevant to the way I am feeling today.

I have been troubled to see a river I knew so well and have fished more than any other look so different. Aside from the appearance of the water – the lack of weed and the opalescent colour – there are changes within the surrounding landscape. Trees and bushes have gone, banks have slipped. Bends have widened and gravel runs are now shallow, silty bays. The wildlife has changed as well. The bank opposite me used to be high and vertical. When I last stood here, a decade ago, at least a dozen holes were dotted along this short stretch – each one home to a pair of sand martins. The parents were busy, in and out with beaks crammed with bugs, and making that lovely, insect-like chatter – similar to the more familiar house martin but with less nasal tone and more bubble. Today, there is not a single squeak.

The martins have certainly suffered from the presence of mink – another North American animal that has flourished in Britain having found an accidental path into our ecology. One summer, when the river was high, I watched a family of mink work their way through the sand martin colony, using the water level to swim from nest to nest. Today, there is no sign of any burrows, though the mink alone are not to blame. The bank itself is eroded, the river running high far more often as our weather becomes more extreme. And perhaps more importantly, there is far less food for the sand martins than there once was. The lack of insect larvae within the water is reflected by the lack of fly life above. The hatches that provided endless food for the birds twenty years ago are now little more than a trickle.

— ✦ —

There I go again. Wallowing in the past. The river has changed, and changed significantly, but there are winners as well as losers. The mink, for example, have been muscled out in recent years by the resurgent otter. And while anglers are anxious about the threat to fish stocks, the otters are also developing quite a taste for signal crayfish. It could be that future generations of otter exist on a diet made up almost exclusively of signal crays, meaning the fish populations can stabilise.

In this respect, Thoreau's mantra about change takes a curious twist. This river – any river – is a living thing and as a result is constantly changing and evolving. The balance of the ecology fluctuates like a panicked stock exchange, leaping and diving in response to every subtlety. Mankind's influence only deepens these waves, and prolongs them. An environment already coping with disease and changes of climate will be stretched to breaking point by pollution, extraction and exploitation. Wherever it is able, though, Nature will find a way to work with what it is left with. Sometimes, sadly, a change will be too great and species are lost, but those that are able to adjust and adapt often come back stronger.

The Kennet will be different tomorrow from how it is today. An indiscernible change perhaps, but in another fifteen years those little differences might be significant. What I must do is accept the fact that a river is ever moving and ever adapting. I am guilty of nostalgia – longing for the place as I remember it.

It is daft, really. If the same piece of river remained constant, then within a relatively short time I would lose interest in it. There was a time on the Kennet when I would fish for an afternoon fully expecting to catch half a dozen barbel with a few nice chub mixed in. I was setting myself up for a fall. Catch what I hoped and I would merely meet my expectations; catch any more and the next time I would expect to do the same. The problem sometimes was that my fishing in those days took on a different intensity. I was in better health – good health – but working full-time. I wanted to fish, yet my opportunities were scarce and when they came I would approach them with the momentum that comes from a busy lifestyle. I would buy whatever bait I felt I needed – a gallon of maggots on occasion – and attack the river. Feeding hard and working hard to whip the fish into a frenzy. It was a successful approach in that I caught lots of fish, but was I really gaining what I desired?

When fellow anglers ask me where I would fish if I could fish anywhere I wanted, I often think that I would like to go back and fish a place I knew well in perfect conditions. Experience what I have already experienced. But such moments are far better left where they were. It is not wrong to reminisce, but it is foolish to chase the same moment.

— ⋖ —

I am sitting now – my back nestled comfortably against a fence post, happily crunching an apple. A skylark is singing high over the meadow on the opposite bank. I squint and stare but cannot find him, though the jangly, fizzing song is one of the loveliest threads of the early summer soundtrack. The songbird crescendo has long since peaked – odd birds have remained on their territory and are still singing, but the woodland and garden birds have little need now for voice. It is definitely a time to turn an ear towards farmland, though. Here, as the green hues are beginning to leave the fields, the birds seem to respond to the gold. Aside from the soaring skylarks, the linnets zing and yellowhammers beg for bread but no cheese. The corn buntings have gone from much of our countryside, but in the Kennet valley reed buntings seem to be faring well. This is a fabulous habitat, something that can be quite hard to believe as the river criss-crosses with the A4 and M4, and trains thunder past on the mainline into Paddington. Much of the shallow river valley is privately owned, and, though often farmed, is left to do as it pleases. And while the sand martins have left this stretch, and thinned elsewhere, other populations along the water-course have increased.

I came up to the Kennet in the winter and couldn't believe the number of water rails, while the red kites lollop their way through the sky overhead as though they never left. Just as the mink have given way to the otters, so the clouds of small tortoiseshell butterflies have abandoned the nettles and instead ringlets and meadow browns flit across the grass tops. This environment is always evolving, and as I consider this fact, I look differently at the water before me.

The last time I fished this swim I caught four barbel in my first four casts, and as I approached the river earlier today I had been reminding myself of that morning. Now, though, I find myself looking at a perfect perch swim. The subtle changes in current and a partially collapsed bank have formed a lovely reed-lined slack. I cannot tell if there is much depth, nor would I necessarily want to fish it until the winter – prime time for perch – but finally I am seeing the river in the present.

Thoreau's words echo once more. The river may seem to be ever changing, but only through our own perception of it. In reality, it is simply reacting to the constraints placed upon it, and all the while it remains a river – it stays the same. Just as I have aged, greyed and expanded since I last fished this swim, so the Kennet has simply altered with time.

8

SIDE STREAMS
AND
DIVERSIONS

The Blackwater

I f the air is still, and I am awake, then every night,
shortly after midnight, comes a low rumble. It is hard
to pinpoint at first, a distant growl that is too subtle to
fully focus upon. After maybe thirty seconds the sound
is clear enough to distinguish, though thereafter the
volume never rises. Instead, there is merely a long, deep
resonance that will often lull me back to sleep. I presume
it is a military aircraft. Perhaps a reconnaissance flight at
high altitude and minimal velocity. It is certainly distant
and – but for the incredible quiet that we live in here –
would pass by unheard.

When Sue and I first came to Dorset, the silence kept us
awake at night. We had moved from a fairly rural location,

but that had been only a short cast from a railway line, and close enough to motorway and main road for us to hear the constant hum of tyres on tarmac. Here, though, there is no passing traffic. In fact, the lane runs out before it reaches our cottage. Instead, tucked away as we are in the hills, the only non-natural nocturnal sound usually comes from the fridge, and in those initial nights of our moving here, it seemed to tap and growl like a bluebottle in a biscuit tin. We quickly acclimatised, and our subconscious minds soon filtered out the unsociable timekeeping of the local cockerels.

Normally, our nights are not disturbed by noise. I will occasionally stir, and if the interruption sounds interesting then I will rouse myself. Last week a badger woke me, snuffling beneath the window a few feet from my head. Of course, I had to peek, and then took an age to get back to sleep. A few winters back an unusual owl hoot nudged me awake, though it didn't call again until the following night. This time I sat up. Again, it stayed silent as soon as I was alert to it, so the following night I vowed to jump out of bed as soon as it began and to try to find the culprit. I haven't heard it since, and were the nights here not so quiet, then I wouldn't have heard it at all.

— ◆ —

It would seem I have been spoiled by four years of silent nights. My ears have got too used to the hush. Right now, as I pause by the riverside, even with the alders and ash in full leaf, the noise from the M27 is deafening. It might not help that I am here without a rod in my hand. Perhaps, when I have fished this river in the past, the direct connection with the water helped to wash away the pounding roar of the motorway. After all, a red-topped float can be quite a distraction. For now, though, I think I'll wander a little further downstream.

The etymology of many of the names of the rivers I have visited is ambiguous at best. As I've mentioned, the Mole, for example, seems not to be named as romantically as it really should, whereas the name 'Kennet' has attracted various arguments as to its derivation. That river was once known as the Cunnit, a name widely accepted to have been taken from the Roman fortification of Cunetio, in the present-day village of Mildenhall. However, historian Michael Dames, who has written extensively about the Neolithic landscape around the Kennet's source, suggests that 'Cunnit' was in fact a variation of a word that would likely cause offence were I to repeat it.

Fortunately, I need not dwell on the point, and instead I return my attention to the water in front of me. I rather think that the naming of this particular stream is somewhat more straightforward: the Blackwater. One of at least a dozen similarly named waterways in the British Isles. There are two in Hampshire – a third if you include the small New Forest stream of Black Water – and this river is well named. It is dark rather than black, but in

Hampshire, a county of sparkling chalk streams, such a course seems out of place.

There is a certain defiance about this river. It rises in Redlynch, just over the Wiltshire border – only a couple of miles away from the bridge upon which I stood gazing into the Hampshire Avon. Not too far downstream from where I find myself today, the river gets swallowed up by the River Test, before slipping between dock cranes and cruise liners into Southampton Water. Amidst this chalk-stream network, the Blackwater flows with an identity very much of its own.

— ∙ —

The great swathe of chalk that forms the downs and plains of Hampshire and Wiltshire is replaced further south by clay and sand. To my west and south, much of this substrate is blanketed by mixed woodland and open heath.

The New Forest was created a thousand years ago when William the Conqueror designated the area as a royal forest. In accordance with Norman practice, forest law prohibited the hunting of wild animals or the destruction or cultivation of the land and plants on which they might feed. For the peasant classes, this created huge restrictions. Traditional sources of food and fuel were gone, and penalties for breaking forest law severe. Many settlements were scrubbed out, the residents evicted, and much of the area has remained property of the Crown ever since. Afforded National Park status in 2005, despite its popularity with walkers, cyclists, naturalists and foragers, the New Forest is one of the most diverse habitats in Europe, retaining its unique identity within one of the most densely populated counties in Britain.

To the west of the New Forest, the Hampshire Avon cuts a careful course, slipping quietly on its way, as if hoping not to be noticed. This tiptoeing seems to work. A few of the Forest streams find it, but most make their own way to the sea – draining the acidity from the bogs and wet heathland without tainting the crisp chalk water of the Avon. And the Blackwater is typical of these waterways. It rises in the north-west corner of the New Forest and then works slowly and steadily east, picking up thick clay-cloyed rivulets as it does so. There is little time for it to gather pace or size so instead the Blackwater snakes quietly, crowded by hawthorn and alder – hiding in the shadows. Dark and mysterious.

— ✦ —

I am thankful that I've been watching where I place my feet – and if the toadling that I have now moved into safer space knew the perils of getting caught beneath a size 11 wellington then he would be thankful too. I'm surprised to find him in this spot. The river is sluggish but I'd never-theless be surprised to see toads spawning in it. The banks are high, which means that access in and out would be tricky and dangerous for them. This particular young toad quite likely emerged from the gravel pit a hundred yards or so to my left, but still it would have had to negotiate a different stream to end up here. It is likely that he was dropped by something which had intended to eat him. Toads do live a perilous life, after all.

A female toad will lay as many as 5,000 eggs in spring, and, of those, only a handful will survive to sexual maturity. Despite being slightly toxic, the toad is under threat from predation throughout its life. Tadpoles are picked off by fish, newts, insects and their larvae; but growing legs and climbing out of the pond only shifts the source of the threat for them. Birds and mammals will always grab an easy meal, and there is the danger of an errant footfall or car tyre to contend with. Small toads, like this chap, need to find somewhere dark and moist where they can hole up and keep safe. Every year, a great mass of young frogs and toads find their way from the lake below our cottage into an enormous compost heap not far from our back gate. That sort of spot would seem a perfect refuge for them, being warm, moist and full of food. One thing it doesn't offer, though, is safety. I have spotted at least a dozen different grass snakes on or around the compost heap this spring, and a grass snake is rather partial to toad.

There are quite a few species that, as a fisherman, I take a little for granted. I have already mentioned kingfishers and water voles in this context, while otters have become so widespread that on some rivers I might enjoy half a dozen sightings in a single afternoon. The grass snake is another such animal. They are fond of water, primarily because their diet consists largely of amphibians. They will take small mammals and young birds on occasion, and even fish, but as ambush predators a slow-moving frog or toad forms perfect prey for them.

Anglers will often see grass snakes – particularly on overgrown ponds or slow-moving rivers and canals. They are superb swimmers, moving through the water as easily as they would on land. I have had plenty of encounters, and just a week or so ago found three basking on a dead log beside a tench lake that I was fishing. It wasn't until I discovered the snakes on my doorstep that I really began to understand them, though.

The British Isles fall in the most northern part of the grass snake's range. There are none in Ireland, of course, after St Patrick's successful eviction, and they only just creep into the southernmost area of Scotland. The main reason for this is climate. Grass snakes are oviparous, and their eggs require a temperature in excess of 22°C in which to incubate. Hence their love of compost, in which the rotting vegetation maintains the necessary warmth.

I love finding them in early spring – fresh from hibernation and sluggish from the cold. Then, they will flatten themselves against my skin, any instinct of fear completely banished by the need to warm their blood. Admittedly, it is somewhat self-centred, but I rather like the sense that I am benefiting a wild animal through touch. Of course, the same snake a couple of months later will slip away as soon as it sees me, but it doesn't stop me looking for them.

— 🐟 —

After another hundred yards the drone of the motorway is distant enough for me to sit down and have my lunch. There is a specific swim that I want to work my way down to, but in the meantime I will content myself with this outlook. Here, there is a short gap in the trees on either bank and the nettles and hogweed have leapt up with the opportunity. I avoid both, and instead nestle in the long grass. It is dry, and the sun warm. Summer will be giving no days back to spring this year. In fact, the wheatear that I saw this morning on the hill behind our cottage would likely have been making his way south again. A failed breeding attempt and little else to stay for.

It is still early in the fishing season, but there is no sign that any anglers have trodden these banks as yet. I am not too surprised, as small river fishing is overlooked by many modern anglers – in fact, there are many who will not fish a river at all. They instead turn to the multitude of managed, cultivated lakes and ponds that have sprung up over the last few decades. Guaranteed bites from hungry fish and a short walk to the water without even getting your trainers dirty. It is convenient and in keeping with the whirlwind of modern society, and I for one don't mind a jot. With fewer anglers, our riverbanks are all the more absorbing.

I feel slightly guilty about using this grassy bank as a cushion, but the growth beneath me is so thick that it should spring back none the worse for its encounter with my backside. I don't know my grasses well, but around me I can see rye grass and cocksfoot. Thankfully, the seed-heavy heads have already delivered the bulk of their pollen. My eyes are itchy, but my nose isn't streaming as it has done in recent weeks. It is always a bind in the early season, and this year seems to be particularly bad.

Suddenly, I am distracted by a flutter of orange. A skipper has landed just a couple of feet from me, its wings folded back like the ears of a chided puppy. It is a large skipper, its wings more marked than on a small, and despite the name it remains a little, oft-overlooked butterfly. Rather like the shift in birdsong, summer sees a change of the guard for the butterflies, and the grassland lovers are now on the wing. Meadow browns, gatekeepers, ringlets and marbled whites. On a still day the meadows are alive with the flutter of wings.

At home, the butterflies have been a benefit to Sue. Every day, regardless of the weather, she walks up the edge of the field opposite the cottage. At first, because of her ill health, she could only manage a couple of dozen yards, but after a year she finally made it halfway along the treeline. Last autumn, she achieved her target: the gate just short of the corner, a perfect leaning post where she could

131

catch her breath for the walk back. From sighting the first brimstone of spring through to the small tortoiseshells caught out by midwinter sunshine, Sue would regularly reach for the butterfly book when she got home. She has totted up eighteen species on her walks, not bad for a field edge, and has got to know one or two quite personally. Her daily footsteps have worked a neat path through the grass and for maybe two months a peacock butterfly would bask on the same spot each day. It would flutter up as Sue approached and settle again as soon as she passed. Those fabulous eyes of shimmering yellow and flashes of blue backed into deep burgundy on the wings of a fresh peacock certainly lift the soul. To recognise one as a familiar beside your toes is a moment that will lift the whole day.

In this gap in the trees, the water below me glows bronze in the sunlight. In the shallow water beside the opposite bank I can make out the larger pieces of shale-like stone on the bottom. It is reminiscent of the Leidle on Mull after rain – the water stained by the peat of the bogs at the head of the valley. There is little here in the way of weed or marginal plants. Instead, the brambles roll down and kiss the surface, swaying rhythmically in the gentle current. I can't see any fish in the shallower water, but in this river, without the thick beds of water crowfoot, the deeper darker water is the safest place to hide when the sun is high.

I could have brought a rod with me today, just for a few casts. There is a spot on the far bank, where the river darkens as it snakes back under cover and the trunk of an alder reaches out into the flow to form a lovely, oily slack. A float would look fantastic as it nudged around the shadows, and who knows what might drag it under. Not a barbel – that's for sure. The fish that dominated my angling for a decade does not swim in the Blackwater. Not yet at least. Barbel have turned up in the Test so perhaps it is only a matter of time before they are 'helped', under the cover of darkness and by human hand, into the Blackwater.

It was this lack of barbel that actually first drew me here to fish. It wasn't just that I had become a single-minded angler, chasing only one species, but I had also begun to complicate my fishing. I had got stuck in a cycle where I couldn't leave anything to chance – I would head off to the Kennet with spare rods and reels, bank sticks and nets; enough bait to catch every fish in the river and enough food to last me a week. No stone lay unturned. My fishing trips were part of the whirlwind. Work, play, weekends away. So many weddings, and stag dos; and we wanted a flat and a mortgage; and when I found the time to fish, I needed to catch and I needed to catch barbel. Today, I recall catching certain fish but I can remember no other details of the capture. Did it rain? Did I even notice? My angling was driven by adrenaline and I needed some balance.

I had crossed over the Blackwater a hundred times while thundering down the motorway to see relatives or to fish the Hampshire Avon; and although the river had always intrigued me I had never come close to fishing it. When I finally found myself on the riverbank with a rod in my hand, I couldn't believe how ready I was for the experience. I had just the bare essentials and half a pint of maggots with me. And before I did anything else, I simply sat and breathed.

I sat, in fact, precisely where I am now.

It is a little more sheltered here. The river curves slightly, allowing me to drop below the top of the bank where the traffic noise is pleasantly muffled. To my left is a smaller stream that meets the Blackwater below my feet. The other stream is chalk-filtered and completely clear, and for many yards runs alongside the cloud of the Blackwater before the dark water prevails. The result is a bizarre two-tone strip of water, with halves that contrast like the keys on a piano. As the two begin to mix, so the darker water billows slowly like smoke, curling menacingly before swallowing up the light.

The crease that forms between the two is a perfect place to place a bait. Fish can lie in the slower, darker water and as food items drift past they can nip out and grab them.

On that first visit, I set up a float rig and a relatively small hook, using a couple of maggots as bait and feeding half a dozen into the water each time I ran the float along the crease. Bites came steadily, first from dace, then roach, and after an hour or so it became a lottery as to what I might hook next. There were gudgeon, perch and chub, and then over three consecutive casts I caught a brown trout, a flounder, followed by a grayling. Two fish of well-oxygenated chalk-stream water sandwiching a sea fish!

Flounder are very tolerant of freshwater and are the principal fish in many estuaries, where they work the mudflats to find marine worms and small crabs. Here, though, the river is non tidal, and still has a couple of weirs to pass before touching saltwater. The flounder must have found its way here by accident – perhaps a combination of a flooded river meeting a spring tide, or maybe as a meal dropped by a passing seagull.

The grayling, on the other hand, will have almost certainly spent its early life in the small chalk stream, and will return to the clear water when it feels the urge to spawn. Grayling require cool, clean water in which to lay their eggs and are not tolerant of low oxygen levels. On the River Kennet their range contrasts neatly with that of the barbel. The grayling thrive in the cold upper reaches where the barbel are unable to prosper, and although the species do overlap, there are relatively few stretches where one would expect to encounter both.

I sometimes feel a little sorry for the grayling. It is a fish striking in appearance, with tiny scales on sleek flanks that glisten aquamarine. Its most notable feature is the huge, sail-like dorsal fin, which is edged in red and delicately spotted. It fights well, and moves in the water with a grace that has earned it the moniker 'The Queen of the Stream'.

Yet the grayling is maligned by some game fishermen, worried that it, like the barbel, may have too keen a taste for salmon eggs, while also competing for river space with more desirable brown trout. As the grayling has an adipose fin, a small seemingly non-functional growth between the dorsal fin and the tail, it is taxonomically grouped with the Salmonidae (salmon and trout), and this is perhaps a reason why many coarse fishermen overlook the species, seeing it as a game fish.

So it is that one of our most beautiful fish swims largely unnoticed by many, although respect and recognition of the species is growing. Their love of cold water means they will feed in the depths of winter, when most other species are inactive. Their omnivorous diet is a bonus for the angler, who can fly-fish for them on a gold-headed nymph or catch them on worms or sweetcorn beneath a float. In parts of Finland, the Sami people believe that the grayling eat gold. It is a belief that was once more widespread across Northern Europe, and likely comes from when grayling are taken for the pot. Their stomachs often contain small, yellow grains that could well be mistaken for tiny nuggets of gold, when in truth they are the pieces of stone used by the caddis larvae to build a shell.

There are nearly 200 species of caddis fly in Britain, and the larvae of most will build protective casings for themselves from small stones, sand and pieces of weed.

Some species can be identified through the particular structure of the casing, whereas others are a little less fussy. The grayling will eat the casing knowing that the larva is inside, but is then unable to digest the materials, and any subsequent analysis of the fish's gut will reveal small fragments of 'gold'.

— ⬩ —

There is sudden panic on the gravel pit on the far bank. The trees and brambles are keeping the water hidden, but a large flock of gulls is suddenly airborne and shouting its disapproval. It is likely a raptor that has put them up, and I duck my head to try and get a better view. The trees are too thick with leaves, though, and the sky overhead too bright to focus within. Still the birds fuss – mainly black-headed gulls by the sound of them – a rasp of discontent, reminiscent of a raucous House during Prime Minister's Questions. They are calming now, though, and settling back on the water. Called back to order.

I look back at the river below me. It is a lovely little pool. The chalk water bubbles in with such an innocence, blissfully unaware that in moments it will be engulfed. And though the Blackwater slips by in an inky darkness, it does so with mystery rather than malevolence. There are so many places to put a bait. The far bank, where the river runs slow and deep, looks good for perch and bream, whereas the tail of the pool, where the water funnels and shallows, is surely thick with dace.

The trail of willow to the far left is where, on our last visit here, my father hooked a clonking chub. He was using his father-in-law's – my late grandfather's – old rod, and the reel sang as the chub dived first for the roots of the willow and then for the sanctuary of the deeper, darker water. It was a fantastic fight, during which I was far more anxious than my unflappable father. He teased and guided the chub, letting the rod tip plunge as it absorbed every thump the fish could muster.

I will come back here one day, with just a rod and reel and a tub of maggots. The Blackwater straightened me out as an angler – stopped me taking it all too seriously. And though I don't feel the need for such counsel now, I would love to cast here again because it would be so much fun.

I smile to myself. At some point the rumble of the motorway had been lost to the soft notes of the stream. I can hear the noise again now, as soon as I consider it, but I sit with a sense of ease that I couldn't have imagined I would find a couple of hours earlier.

It's time to get back on the road now though and rejoin the throng. When I last left this place, Sue and I were homeowners with pension plans and a car apiece. Sue had just become Chartered in Personnel Development, and our savings account swelled by the month. It seems a very long time ago now.

9

STRIPPING BACK

The Little Weir

Of all the places I have revisited, and all the waters I have sat beside, nowhere has felt quite so bittersweet as the wooden picnic table upon which I now sit. Sue and I sat together here seven years and a season ago to steal half an hour from a day that was already ours. The whirlwind of our wedding had left us pleasantly shell-shocked – all these people and all this fuss just for us. Yet we'd barely snatched a moment together, and it was nice to have a few minutes to reflect and ruminate – to simply catch up.

It was also probably the longest time I've spent beside a river without gawping at it. Sue was already becoming poorly, though we put her failing health down to stress and exhaustion. The wedding seemed to knock the wind from her sails, and while it is an occasion recalled with great fondness, it is also a reminder of the onset of her illness.

The years since have seen us stripped down to almost nothing. Sue has lost her job and career. We had little choice but to sell our flat and use every penny of our savings. Our clothes are the same, just well worn, and we have learned to cut one another's hair. Life isn't bad, just different, and perspective is always on hand to give us faith in what we do still have. Since the wedding, three of our guests have become ill and not recovered, while others have had their lives turned upside down.

Yet Sue and I still have each other and there is the realistic hope that Sue's health will steadily improve. Rather as I lamented the state of the River Kennet before accepting that it just didn't tally with my sentiments about it, if we accept life as it is in the moment, there is always something positive to find.

Only this week, Sue and I were sitting on our steps with a cup of tea in the afternoon sun. Black ants were busy between the paving slabs beneath our feet, tidying and digging. The soil was dry and loose, and a small group seemed to be excavating a new burrow. They were fascinating to watch. One particular ant seemed to drag out only the largest lumps. Really straining to get them above ground and out of the way. Another focused on tiny fragments, and seemed very considered in the way it placed them on the paving. A third was frenetic – dashing in and out of the hole but knocking as many pieces in as it brought out. We drained our mugs and after a while we spoke about what we had been watching. Our thoughts were similar. We agreed the ants were effectively working as one, as colonial insects are inclined to do, yet these few individuals operated in distinctly different ways from one another. Which of them, therefore, made the decisions? Or did they instinctively know exactly which role and what action to take? Were they thinking as one, working together as one – or just reacting in kind to the precise conditions of the moment? Or were we simply being guilty of anthropomorphism – of attributing to the ants human traits or behaviour that simply weren't there? The ants might have been swapping roles and behaving differently dependent on the size of particle they were carrying.

An afternoon cup of tea had taken a lovely sideways slant due to the actions of a half dozen insects. We didn't want answers and we haven't dwelt on the moment since, but ten years or so ago we probably wouldn't have even noticed the ants were there. We had money and worked hard to earn it, but lived a life of ferment, caught in the trappings of the material world. We needed nice things to justify the stress we endured to earn them. We were forever planning – for holidays, parties and weekends away. We might have taken a moment to look at busy ants, but only if we had stepped sideways to find them.

I am reminded again of Thoreau's mantra, or perhaps more poignantly the words of my friend, Chris Yates: 'You can't buy a moment,' he once told me. Today, we might spend our lives looking sideways – glancing up at soaring buzzards and down at excavating ants – and this is fine providing we can also stand still. But therein lies the tricky part: in this modern world it is almost impossible to stand still.

— ⋙ —

A moorhen has just ambled out of the reeds beside me, tail flicking, and then panics as it suddenly notices I am here. It makes no sound – perhaps suggesting that it has no chicks to warn of my presence – but it almost falls over as it spins on those long, gangly green toes.

Before me is the Little Weir, which, as the name suggests, carries a small side stream away from the main river. This is a very well known stretch of the River Kennet, and I have spent many, many hours at this particular spot. For a long time I barely gave it a second glance, and instead joined the throng of anglers jostling for the prime barbel swims on the main river downstream. The weir pool here is a reasonable size but much of it is shallow, and from a quick glance, particularly in summer with water level low, there doesn't seem to be much water to target. This belief is supported by the tail of the pool, which shallows to mere inches before bubbling through a narrow, pebbled reach that is barely deep enough to wet your toes.

Having had my angling mind straightened out by a trip to the River Blackwater, I decided to come and fish this pool in a similar manner. I knew I would almost certainly have it to myself – it is barely fished – and the prospect of taking with me only a few basic pieces of tackle, rather than crushing the car's rear suspension, was really appealing. When I first came here, I brought with me a few slices of bread and half a pint of maggots, put up a rod beside the car and had fun. From the first cast I was bombarded with minnows, but soon other fish arrived: dace, roach, and gudgeon. I landed a pike, which snatched a small fish as I reeled in, and then hooked a lovely chub of nearly five pounds. Two much smaller chub followed, before the rod was almost wrenched from my grip as a much bigger fish made a lunge for the head of the pool. Within a couple of seconds the line fell limp as the hook straightened. It could only have been a barbel.

Of course, I expected similar good luck on my next visit, but thankfully fishing is never quite so predictable. The next time, I came with barbel in mind and didn't get a bite. There was perhaps a touch of arrogance on my part to think that I need only turn up with suitable tackle and bait and the fish would respond.

For my third attempt, I left the tackle in the car and just took myself and a pair of polarised glasses to the riverbank. It certainly opened my eyes. Often, when met with a small stream or pool, it is easy to assume that any fish present will find a bait wherever you place it. As I learned on the Blackwater, though, a subtle feature might be thick with fish, while a foot to the left there is not a fin to be seen. That crease between clear and dark water on the Blackwater was an obvious spot, but sometimes a depression in the riverbed or a slight deflection in the current can be so subtle that you only find it by accident.

This is where watching the water is so beneficial. Not only should you look to identify fishy-looking lies, but also look for areas that won't hold fish. A reed-lined bay might look enticing, but if the water is shallow and the bottom thick with silt, the oxygen levels will be lower than in the main flow. There will be less weed growth, fewer invertebrates and fewer fish. Disregarding that whole area will heighten your focus upon the areas where the fish might actually be.

The weather today is similar to that third visit. The sun is high and strong, with just some broken cloud to soften the light occasionally. The water quality, as I found when I was further downstream, is very different. With my polarised glasses taking the sheen from the water's surface, I can still make out the larger stones on the bottom, but the water is only a few feet deep and I should be able to see the edges of every pebble. I am drawn, inevitably, to the twin alders on the far bank – just above the pool's tail. There the water moves just as I remember and I smile as I recall the endless fish that seemed to dwell in that short run. It is best viewed from the far bank, and, judging by the mass of hogweed and meadowsweet, no one has stepped on that side of the pool for some time.

— ❮❮ —

The alder is one of the most familiar trees on British riverbanks. They are lovers of wetland, where they will often dominate the arboreal make-up. They grow quickly but do not grow particularly large or old; a mature specimen might measure sixty or seventy feet and live little longer than a man. While they may not have the thick trunk and reptilian bark of a 500-year-old oak, they do have their own curious charm. The fruits grow on long stalks, and remain on the tree through the winter. The branches look flimsy, but are master snaggers of stray fishing lines. In a popular fishing spot, an alder might resemble a Christmas tree come the end of the season – festooned with floats and lead weights. And even the most nimble-limbed angler will struggle to retrieve his tackle from the sticky-leaved higher branches. The alder will often have multiple trunks, which provide plenty of footholds for the first few feet of a climb, but the higher branches are often slim and whippy – certainly too weak for an angler to inch along.

The most impressive feature of an alder, though – certainly as far as an angler is concerned – lies at its base. Here, the tree produces adventitious roots that finger their way out of the trunk and reach sideways and down. This is the ideal trick for a plant to master if it finds itself growing on a slippery riverbank where the water might try to unearth it from below. With roots reaching horizontally back into the bank, the alder can almost 'lean' out across the river. If the river is too deep to negate, those appendages that look for grounding on the river side of the trunk will often reach out and then fold back in under themselves. Over time, as more and more roots start protruding, an alder thus creates a 'raft', beneath which lies a sanctuary for fish.

Here, beside the little weir, two trees grow side by side, creating the perfect area for fish to lie. The root mass is so established that I am able to stand upon it without the slightest creak, knowing that beneath my feet is a lovely cave, full of fish. Within water, even dead alder does not rot, but instead hardens like rock. Mankind has long made use of this property, and in ancient times crannogs – the fortified dwellings that were built on the lochs and marshlands of Ireland and Scotland as long as 5,000 years ago – were often placed on top of alder trunks, safe in the knowledge that the buildings would not disappear beneath the water. Here, on the Little Weir, my needs are purely piscatorial, but it is reassuring to know that I can step onto the root mass with little fear of getting wet.

The main current of the pool pushes across to this point, with some of the water deflecting sideways into a large back eddy and the rest slipping gently beside the alders. Any food items brought down by the weir will drift past a mass of hungry mouths, providing plenty of meals for minimal risk. With this in mind, I would reckon that there must be moments when 90 per cent of the body mass of fish in this pool squash themselves into this one spot, which itself holds less than one per cent of the water in the weir. In such prime locations, fish will literally squeeze themselves together like sardines in a tin – with the bigger and stronger fish in the prime spots and their smaller cousins grabbing whatever space is left. There will be all sorts of species here too. Predators will cosy up beside prey. Pike and perch fin to fin with dace and gudgeon. Undisturbed, they will remain like this for hours on end, only moving in response to lowering light levels or an urge to feed.

That first time I crept around to this point, the potential almost made my eyes pop out. I had cast towards the top of this run on that first successful dangle in this pool, but had tried my luck in a few different places as well. Now, though, I realised that this was *the* spot. I nipped back to the car, grabbed a tub of maggots, and then trickled a few through the gaps in the root mass before setting my eyes on the water immediately behind the raft. A couple of maggots drifted down beneath me but vanished in a flash of silver. I fed another handful into the water and watched as dace and roach darted after them. Then the chub started to respond. They were reluctant to leave the shelter of their roof, but a couple couldn't resist following the loose bait out into the open and soon I had a half a dozen competing just a few feet from me. They were good fish, all over four pounds, and were quick to muscle out the smaller fish. I was rapt – and wondered what else might be tempted out. Instead, though, the chub seemed to prickle at something, and while they didn't panic, they started moving much more warily.

A pike slowly drifted out from beneath the bank. Not huge, but big enough to cause some anxiety. As I watched, another fish nudged up behind it. For a moment, I didn't recognise what it was. Such was its bulk that I expected it to be a carp or salmon. Then, though, as it drew alongside the pike, I realised I was looking at a huge chub. It was tatty and battle-scarred and had a slightly crooked spine – but what a fish! Far bigger than any of the others and far bigger than any other chub I had ever seen. I slipped back away from the water, my heart thumping. I had to cast for it – I had to catch it.

I didn't hook it that day, though I caught plenty of others, but I saw that chub a few times thereafter and finally, on one occasion, it was on the end of my line.

— ⋯ —

The long, slightly pained mew of a red kite draws my ears away from the water. My eyes aren't turned immediately, however; instead, they peek over the top of the Polaroids and scan the surface of the pool for a raptor-shaped reflection. A competing interest in avian life can be a hindrance when looking at water, especially when watching a float. Your eye muscles slow when they have been fixed for a long period, staring at the water, and glancing skyward, even on a cloudy day, can dazzle like midnight lightning. After a few moments of visual adjustment, the bird whose call you responded to is long gone, and almost inevitably you turn back to a float that has moved an inch while you weren't paying attention to it. As a result, I learned from an early age that while fishing I should look to distinguish reflections and shadows rather than rely on seeing the bird itself.

There is no sign of the kite, though, and without a float to monopolise my concentration, I look away from the water to find the culprit. My eyes are immediately distracted by something else. Only fifty or sixty yards behind me, a barn owl is quartering the meadow, seemingly too intent on finding prey to worry about my presence. I have often seen barn owls hunting here, though normally at dusk. The fact that this bird is looking for food on a sunny, summer's afternoon suggests that it has young and that the rewards of nocturnal hunting are none too consistent.

The summer has been unsettled up till now, and cool. Bright days like today have come but always on the back of a stiff breeze, often northerly, and with the promise of wet weather to follow. Although it might seem late in the year for barn owls still to be nesting, it is typical behaviour of the species. They are reactive to the food sources available, and reliant on small rodents, particularly voles, to sustain a brood. If the local vole population explodes in late spring, then some barn owls may well decide to have a second brood. These are birds vulnerable to cold weather and a severe winter can see populations crash. To balance against this, they must flourish while they can and sometimes make for prey while the sun shines.

It is a reflection of the red kite's relative profusion today that, having reacted to that initial call, I have since been entirely focused on the barn owl that in turn caught my attention. The kite has called again, and I can pick it out, perched high in one of the trees (a poplar?) that line another stream beyond the meadow's edge. It is no surprise to see it there – a pair was nesting in that copse on my last visit – but as I mentioned during my trip to Exmoor, such a sighting would have been extraordinary in the very recent past. Of course, watching a barn owl hunt in broad daylight is a treat in itself, and its appearance was likely the cause of the kite's call, but had I seen the kite in the reflection of the pool, would I have turned to look at it?

Suddenly, the barn owl swoops down, turning on those balsa-wood wings and thumping into the grass. It remains down there for some moments, long enough to snack on a grasshopper, before rising up and floating off upriver.

— ✦ —

Until this point in my journey, each river that I have revisited has been at a location a little further on its own journey to the sea. It seems that as I have aged, so I have found myself drifting along with the current, and regardless of the river, I would always find myself further downstream. Today, though, not only am I back on the Kennet, but I am some way upstream of the stretch that I previously walked. I have spent more time fishing the River Kennet than any other river, and though this demonstrates the depth of the relationship I developed with her, it also reflects a time of my life when I had plenty of opportunity to enjoy angling. I could afford to join angling clubs with miles of water to explore and I could afford to drive an hour each way to do so. My bait tubs were always full and my tackle bag bursting. In those days, I would stop somewhere for breakfast and take my pick of the pasties from the little shop in Aldermaston.

And then came the uncertainty. Not just the financial aspect – but the reality of disappearing for a day and leaving a poorly wife at home. As our lives slowed down so did my angling. For too long I had been rushing – fishing at the same pace as my life, and always looking to see what was beyond the next bend. As I blinked myself back into the present moment I found myself heading back upstream, retreading banks I had previously rushed down. By looking back and, more importantly, looking sideways, I began to find pools such as this one. While the fish had always been here, I had not yet been ready to cast for them.

There is a small corner beside the weir sill which epitomises my adjusted sight. Even when I had fished the little weir half a dozen times I hadn't given the spot any close attention. But one day I looked more closely.

The currents immediately beneath a weir sill do not act in the ways suggested by the torrent on the surface. The white water on the surface impacts the upper layers but then rolls out into the pool; while the lower layers of water that remain behind dig into the bottom and often carve out an undercut where food items and fish will collect. The water beneath this sill is no different, though in winter the odd branch will find its way over the weir and wedge itself solid. The back eddy that sweeps around the shallow reedy bay meets an undercurrent created beside the weir, and over time the two currents have bored a deep hole beneath the bank. The depth in this particular corner beside the weir sill drops sharply from around three feet down to five – and, with a thick bramble roof, forms a perfect spot for a barbel.

I mentioned that the bulk of fish in this pool are most likely to be found around the twin alders at the pool's tail, but it is rare that there isn't at least one barbel tucked up in the quiet of this corner. When I first put a bait there – a big lump of luncheon meat with just a single shot to help it to the bottom – I waited less than two minutes before the rod thumped round. With an eight-pounder safely netted, I fished on but didn't have another bite. That seemed to be the pattern: one bite, often within moments, but nothing thereafter. As a result, I would only fish the spot occasion- ally and normally only in pursuit of an all but guaranteed fish on an otherwise fruitless day.

The corner did, though, make for an excellent spot to recommend to others. When Ben, my brother-in-law, fancied catching a barbel I suggested he gave the corner swim a go. It was winter, and the river was high and cold, so it took a little longer for the bite to come; but come it did, and Ben caught a lovely fish of around five and a half pounds. My brother Richard fared even better when he had a go the following autumn. He missed the first bite but unusually got a second chance and landed a stunning fish after quite a fight; at nine pounds eleven ounces, it was a superb first barbel.

Against my advice, Richard persevered for another in the same spot, and I was shocked when an hour later he was into another fish. This time, however, the fish was too quick for him, and dived behind a submerged stump, seemingly lost. I took the rod for a moment, just to check, and after a little teasing the tip gave a gentle kick. I applied steady pressure, letting the rod gently ease the fish out, and soon a firmer thump suggested the fish was free. I passed the rod back to Rich and he worked the barbel into open water and continued the fight. It was a lovely long, lean fish, without a blemish to fin or scale, and weighed eleven pounds eleven ounces. My brother hasn't been barbel fishing since – he probably thinks it's too easy.

While I pointed others into the corner swim, I focused my own attention on the run beneath the alders – and that huge chub. The fishing was fabulous, some of the very best I have experienced. And what made it so good was the seemingly endless fish that were there to be caught. There is no fun in catching the same fish over and over again, yet the cast of this little weir pool seemed to change by the week. Away from the chub I caught perch to nearly three and a half pounds, and barbel to over fourteen pounds; and though some of the fish, especially the chub, would have met me more than once, the vast majority didn't.

— ◆ —

And so to that monster ...

I saw the enormous chub twice more in the water, on each occasion at a point in time where I wondered if she had left the pool or swum her last. It was early autumn when I finally hooked her, on an afternoon where the little weir was in particularly generous mood.

I had bites immediately that day, with an initial run of small fish interrupted by a brace of nice bream. I had caught small bream in the pool before but these were big-backed, mature fish of four or five pounds. Then the chub moved out from the alder cave, and I caught four good fish in quick succession before the swim went quiet. I thought a pike must have stirred and shrunk the shoal back beneath the root mass, but out of the blue the rod kicked and I was into another fish. It was heavy and too powerful to be a chub, and on light tackle I had to be as careful as I was able.

After ten minutes, the fish began to tire and I worked it slowly across the current, kicking off my boots and slipping into the water to get better purchase. Then all went solid. The fish had ducked behind a rock in mid-river and wedged the line. I could see it, or at least its tail, and could wade comfortably to it. As I edged closer, though, it shook its head and threw the hook, before sliding back across into the darker water.

It looked to have been a barbel of at least twelve pounds and for some minutes I just sat, heart pounding, letting the adrenaline ease.

I fished on and caught two other barbel, both around eight pounds, before bites again slowed. I decided to try and get the chub moving again, feeding lots of maggots and putting on a tiny, size 20 hook. Chub are, in the words of Izaak Walton, author of the 1653 work *The Compleat Angler*, the *fearfulest of fishes*, and though there are days when they will engulf a great black slug or a bunch of worms, on others they are desperately wary. They will pick a bait up very gently in their lips and drop it should they feel the slightest resistance.

The rod bent round again, and another heavy fish kicked slowly in the current. This was no barbel, and for a few moments I wondered what I had hooked, before realising I knew *exactly* what I had hooked. Gently now, Kev, gently …

It was painstaking, with every lunge tightening the knot in my stomach. I was desperately trying to relax, fearing that my rigidity might reflect in the action of the rod and jar the hook free. After some minutes, however, the chub began to circle ever closer, until finally it surfaced and opened a huge pair of white-lined lips, big enough to mouth a tennis ball, with my absurdly small hook nicked lightly in the top.

As I drew it over the net, the hook hold gave, the rod sprang straight, and time slowed almost to a standstill. The biggest chub I had ever seen was halfway over the rim of my net, momentum bringing it towards me. If I waited a second it would be mine. But I didn't. I panicked – lunged and lifted, and turfed the fish back into the water. For a moment it sat below me, enormous, before drifting slowly back across the gravel to the sanctuary of the alders.

I never saw it again.

10

CONTENTMENT

Parr's Pool

For the angler, the view from a bridge can be infuriating. There will be plenty of water to look at, but the best bits – the undercuts and shadows – are just out of sight. The dark water beneath the structure is also somewhere you long to see deeper into, and many's the angler who has lost his hat from leaning too far over a precipice in order to glimpse an extra fin or two.

As you may have gathered by now, I have spent a lot of hours standing on a lot of bridges, and the view from this particular one is as good as any other. It's helped by the fact that there is little more than a trickle beneath me and that, this being a side stream controlled by a hatch, the bridge was built with little clearance over the watercourse – safe in the knowledge that the water will rarely swell with any serious menace. A couple of willows sit either side of the pool, their wispy branches meeting and mingling. While they don't exactly form an arch, the canopy closes in tightly and the leaves weave together like the wicker of a creel. I am facing west, and the sun normally illuminates the head of the pool, filtering through the water at an angle that seems to light up the fish from below.

This is a place where I would usually stand in the winter months, and what little sunlight there is today is high, it being summer, and making no direct impression on the water below. It has made little impact on my ability to see the fish, though. As always, the view from this bridge is filled with fins.

I am still on the Kennet – or at least, a side stream of it. This spot is some twenty miles upstream of the Little Weir, and here the river valley is wide, with a network of streams, ditches and rivulets all flowing for the same cause. This particular trickle begins life with some ambition. Two hundred yards or so upstream of the bridge, it rolls off the main river course and swirls proudly around the pool with the hatch, digging deep into the gravel before powering off with purpose. Within yards, the stream narrows, although it retains a steady depth until this point, where, suddenly, it runs out of oomph.

If I were sixteen and had a decent run-up, I think I could comfortably jump the pool upstream from this bridge, but downstream I wouldn't need to worry: I could wade across without getting my ankles wet and, although it does widen once more, it seems to be aware, much like the stream back at Eype, that its own course is a short one.

The trees here offer the only extensive cover for the fish, and the willow at the head of the pool trails its branches into the water, stalling the flow and creating a shadowed slack behind. Although the water here carries the same milky tinge that I saw downstream, the impact isn't quite so severe, and the lack of depth means I can see the riverbed quite comfortably. Looking through my binoculars, I could be staring into an aquarium.

Immediately below me, where the stream riffles and shallows, three brown trout skate sideways across the current, while above them, in the quieter water, lie half a dozen chub. The largest of these must be nudging five pounds, a big fish for such a small stream, and the others are all over three pounds. Roach drift alongside the chub, and a small shoal of dace skit about in the slightly stiffer current to the right. I can see four or five perch, but they are all fairly small and I had hoped to see one or two of their larger cousins. It is, after all, the perch that I tend to target on this little stream.

— ❮❰ —

I once read a piece by a specimen angler (I do not remember his name) who said that he had no interest in fishing a water unless he knew it held a bigger fish than he had previously caught. I respected his candour: big fish were his passion and breaking records and reaching landmarks his drive. I was also curious; if he went fishing and didn't achieve a new personal best, did he go home dissatisfied?

Did it matter where he fished – would he happily wet a line in an inner city slum or beside a Heathrow runway if he might catch a monster? Or would he pass up a chance to fish a stunning piece of water like this one because it wouldn't yield a trophy fish?

Perhaps his priorities have changed since he made the statement, much like my own. The less opportunity I had to fish, the further I retreated upstream. And I rather liked it. I first started exploring stretches of water like this at a time when Sue and I needed to move house and get off the property ladder before debt threw us off. The clutter in the fishing cupboard needed clearing, and bait stocks thinning. Catching big fish started to matter much less than being in a place where time slowed down – where I wouldn't be competing for bank space with other anglers and where the moments between bites meant more than the bites themselves.

In more recent years, Sue and I have had to learn to trust to life. It isn't easy. Money dwindles, opportunities dry up, and yet, if we do our bit – live simply and keep hoping – then somewhere a door always seems to open. And it's been similar with my angling. My friend Peter Arlott introduced me to this particular piece of water and then, as I explored both my new attitude and new water, serendipity smiled sweetly for me. Through the generosity and good nature of others, chances came for me to fish further stretches of the Kennet, including places only normally available to those with money to burn, and even a few spots where anglers don't usually set foot.

With miles of water to explore, I started to travel light. Just the bare essentials – rod, reel, bait, net and kettle. Pockets full and eyes open, I came to lose myself.

— ✦ —

A pike has slowly drifted down the pool and now lies in the quiet water to my left. It is not a particularly big fish, certainly no heavier than the biggest chub in the shoal, but the roach and dace were quick to shrink into the shadows. Perhaps stirred by the movement of the small fish, a large perch has also emerged. It looks stunning. Thick stripes and spiky red fins standing proudly to attention. It is as impressive as the fish I watched that day on the Itchen, and probably half a pound heavier. It seems oblivious to me, as all the fish in the pool do. Despite being only twenty feet away, my form is lost against the wooden patchwork and bricks of the bridge. Also, of course, my presence is benign. I might be looking for fish but I have no intention of casting for them. In fact, I have never cast from the tail of this little pool. I have fished from above, and run a float down as close to the trailing branches as I dare. I have caught chub and perch doing so, but once a couple of fish have been fooled the remainder sink back and cannot be tempted back out. Perhaps I should have double-bluffed them – stood here with a rod and a fierce determination. They would sense me then and move upstream where a different version of me, this one casual and indifferent, would be making a crafty cast.

I have never fished this area at this time of year, though. This particular stretch is open only to trout fishermen at present, and though I would love the chance to cast a fly here – there are some stunning brown trout, and plenty of less beautiful, reared and stocked rainbows – the cost of a permit is far beyond my current means. And while it is lovely to see this valley on a summer's day like this one, it is in winter that I am most compelled to spend time here.

There is a pleasant sense of oversight about this part of Berkshire. Much of the population of this county live in the centre or east of the region, with towns such as Reading, Wokingham and Slough dominating both the landscape and demographic. Head west of Newbury, though, and everything changes. The towns become villages, villages become farms. Cars slow and wood smoke curls from cosy cottages. It is as though a sleepy veil has been laid softly across the world.

To my south is the railway and to the north the A4, but both are mere sideshows to a Kennet masterpiece. The river is never particularly large, but it demands big open spaces which it fills with side shoots and winter excess. The stretch a little further downstream from this bridge is known as The Wilderness, and if you find yourself walking the bank on a cold winter morning, the name could not be more appropriate. The land there is wide and flat, and as the water table rises in response to the rain of autumn, so the meadows become lagoons and the teal flock in their hundreds. The woodland, thick with those wetland-loving alders, fills with water and just a few ridges of earth provide dry passage for the deer and fishermen. The mist forms early in the evenings during the cold months, and the leafless branches twist like the legs of spiders in a cloud of silk. The silence can be almost torturous, particularly when pierced with the pained screams of the water rails. Who needs to catch fish in such a place?

It is odd to consider that despite its wild and untamed appearance, the landscape through this part of the Kennet valley has been heavily influenced by humanity, and much of it by just one man. The eighteenth century found Britain in a state of flux. The Industrial and Agricultural Revolutions saw rapid and radical changes that created the platform for modern society today, but which also accelerated class divisions, which in turn led to civil unrest. With this came the Georgian love of the arts, the work of the Romantic Poets, Coleridge, Wordsworth and Byron, and the architecture that still shapes many of our urban outlooks.

The rural landscape was also changing. Fields became larger, crops were rotated, and machines began replacing manual labour. Country estates were sought after by the wealthy and the accompanying lands and gardens a demonstration of decadence. This was landscape gardening on an epic scale and the work of one particular parkland pioneer was especially favoured.

The influence of Lancelot Brown can still be found across England and parts of Wales. His tendency to suggest to landowners that their estates possessed 'capability' for landscape improvement led to his more familiar moniker, Capability Brown. He was a designer in demand, and his fondness for designs that included open grassland, wooded rides and sweeping lakes became his benchmark, Stourhead being a perfect example. Brown liked his designs to possess a sense of interminability, incorporating sunken borders, ha-has and hatches rather than high fences or hedge lines. To create lakes, Brown would often divert streams from a main river source (such as the Kennet), which would then be dammed. While he did not maintain records of his own, at least 150 of his 'landscapes' remain today – largely faithful to his original design. A revival of appreciation for his work in the early twentieth century saw much restoration and imitation, and many of us will be familiar with his work even though we may not realise it.

Brown's intentions were not piscatorially based, but anglers have certainly benefited from them. Away from the tench-filled lakes beside the manor houses, estate owners began to exploit the less tameable habitats. Shooting and fishing became big business; and by manipulating the rivers more land could be made accessible. The hatches and slips that still criss-cross this flat valley help drain the land between. Water levels can be regulated, and although there will be times, particularly in winter, when much of the ground is underwater, for much of the year it can be used for grazing, stalking and game rearing. While the river is stocked with additional trout to attract fly anglers throughout the summer, the side streams hold plenty of surprises.

— ⋖ —

I've walked a couple of hundred yards upstream, where the run-off from the hatch pool creates a shallow, reed-lined slack. I am not sure why, but there has been a large deposit of silt since my last visit, and the nature of this pool has changed. The same seems to have happened to my right, just below the brambles, where a stout hawthorn stands guard over a small back eddy. In seasons past, these two spots were as reliable as any on the whole fishery. The hawthorn swim in particular used to almost guarantee a big perch or two. The water deepened slightly here, and a float would sit quite still just off the current.

A few seasons ago, when the perch population was still booming, Chris and I would have to toss a coin to see who would have first cast. On one occasion, having success-fully called tails, I readied to cast while Chris made his way up to the reedy bay. Before he had got there, my float had slipped under and I had a two-pounder in the net. 'Your turn!' I called. And Chris caught his own big perch within another couple of minutes.

However, the fishing within the bay would depend on whether or not the Queen of the Stream was present. There are normally a good few pike resident in this short stretch, but there was one big female that would either lay up here or around fifty yards away, downstream under a bed of watercress. It was in the latter spot where a friend, Mick 'Demus' Canning, once hooked her while fishing for perch. He landed her too, on four-pound breaking strain line, and she weighed over eighteen pounds.

A pike that size can be a dominant distraction in this small piece of water, though, and I have caught many fish here on the days she's been away. The water is well oxygenated, coming off the tail of the hatch pool, and as a result is teeming with minnows and gudgeon, which, in turn, attract the perch and pike. It isn't just sub-surface predators who feed here, however. Herons are regular visitors and a few winters back I crept into the reeds and nearly stepped on a bittern. It was the first bittern I had ever seen, and I'm not sure which one of us was more surprised.

— ⋙ —

According to the chimes of the local church, it is lunchtime. Kintbury has two sets of chiming bells that strike several minutes apart. Seeing as I don't carry a watch, I have no idea which set is more accurate, but being an angler, I always take more notice of the second peel – those extra moments can make quite a difference.

Although it is served by the mainline railway route into London, Kintbury maintains a gentle, sleepy feel. This was once a bustling market town, though it became superseded by nearby Hungerford, while in the late eighteenth century Kintbury was boosted by the construction of the Kennet and Avon Canal. Being a mile or two off the A4, the main thoroughfares of the town remain the railway and the canal, and the town moves accordingly. There are brief, express flurries of activity as the school gates open or people rush to and fro from work, but in between times the town runs at the pace of a gently chugging narrowboat.

And four miles to the west, Hungerford has to cope with the choke of through traffic and diesel-driven deliveries, as the market stalls now compete with chain stores and supermarkets. Not that the town suffers too much for it. Hungerford is busy, but the skyline of the High Street will have changed little in centuries, and although the people will never come to terms with the tragic events that took place there in 1987, when a rampaging gunman destroyed so many lives, the town epitomises the enduring quality of the Upper Kennet valley.

A deep, distant hum quickens into a helicopter-rotor-like thump. The lead engine of a high speed train slams past, with a second whistling its way behind. I have ridden this train line a few times before and always ensure I am on the 'northern' side in order to optimise the view of the river. There is a fabulous glimpse of the weed rack on The Wilderness, which was swarming with big perch a couple of winters back. It is a spot known to many, made famous on celluloid in *A Passion for Angling* nearly a quarter of a century ago, though fished by few. As the train rattles on, my eyes always dart through the trees and beneath the brambles for tantalising flashes of water. It is hard to pick out specific swims, but instead I will spy an alder or a twist in a hedge line and let my imagination fill in the gaps. At one point, a little way after the train has hurtled through Kintbury station, comes a moment when I can look straight down the float line of the most perfect swim I have ever fished. The image is so brief, but my eyes take a snapshot which my mind then spends several seconds absorbing. The view I have had from the train is better than the one I have today, here on the ground.

Whenever I squelch across this meadow in winter, I always need to watch my feet. The courses of the drainage ditches are marked by the tufts of club rushes – rather like those that trace the first, sub-surface trickle at Stourhead. But here and there the water slips sideways into the soft grass, creating patches of bog just deep enough to snatch a welly. Then there are the snipe, which tuck up tight to the ground as you approach, only to zip out from under your feet, knocking you off balance through sheer surprise.

There are no snipe here today, though. Instead, the meadow is dry and surprisingly bare. The club rushes are still evident – just. Many have been flattened by bovine hooves, and the cows have provided plenty of new hazards for my feet to avoid.

If I didn't already know that there was a tiny little carrier cutting up the fence line, I might not look to see. The thick sedge beds are a bit of a giveaway, but there are so many ditches and damp depressions that it is easy to get complacent. This, though, is a true carrier. A trickle of water sneaks out of a side stream and cuts a low-profile path back to the main river. With a low flow for most of the year, this carrier gets backed up at the point where it rejoins the Kennet and certainly doesn't appear to be feeding itself. Unless you were to work deep into the sedge on the off-chance, you wouldn't find the water-course by accident – not at its summer level.

My first investigations here were serendipitous. I had been walking the side stream and, having found it losing its oomph, decided to take a shortcut back to the main channel. I stepped through a gap in the undergrowth precisely where the little carrier slipped off the side stream and formed a shallow pool. I reasoned that my easiest passage would be to get into the water and wade as far as I was able. Even though the tangle of brambles and bindweed spilled over the banks and trailed into the water, for fifty yards or so I could work my way unhindered. Then, the course twisted sharply to the right and a young alder blocked my route. I managed to work my way around it, but just as I was about to clamber back down, a flash of silver caught my eye. The water was shallow – no more than eight inches deep – but a few yards downstream was thick with fish. They were dace, and, though not large, must have numbered at least fifty. A little further, where the water level began to threaten the top of my boots, I spied a roach. I climbed up onto the right-hand bank, which was relatively clear at this point, and found a gap in the sedge through which I peered into the water. Within a minute roach were ghosting past. They were reasonable fish with plenty around the half-pound mark. Then a couple of pounders eased beneath my nose, followed by a fish twice the size.

I moved another ten yards and found three bream, one of which must have weighed over five pounds and was longer than the ditch was wide. The bream were quick to spook and I didn't see them again, despite settling down and watching the water for a couple of hours. The roach were there in number, though, with a couple of fish among them being well over two pounds. I was itching to have a cast, but had left my fishing rod way back upstream. I would either have to go back the way I came, or head further down and hope to find a bridge. In the end, I opted for the latter. I *had* to have a cast.

— ⋯ —

An explosion of song bursts from the hawthorn to my left. I cannot see the culprit, but it can only be a Cetti's warbler. Few other birds announce their presence with such alacrity, and it is a song that has not long been heard in the Kennet valley. A non-migratory warbler, the Cetti's was a vagrant in Britain until the early 1970s, when it first bred here. Over the decades, the population has increased, but numbers suffer during a severe winter, and the birds are unusual north of The Wash.

Beneath the hawthorn comes a gentle splash – more of a 'plop' really. It can only be a water vole, a familiar sight in this swim, and a familiar companion when I regularly fished this spot – if I didn't see him then I would likely hear him, gnawing away beneath my toes. The spot itself came to be known as 'Parr's Pool'; as I'd introduced him to the pool, Chris christened it with my name shortly after taking his fourth two-pound perch of the afternoon. The main reason for the label was to ease future conversation, although Parr's Pool is called this name only by a handful of people.

The naming of swims makes life much more straightforward when describing your day in detail to a fellow angler: 'I started in the Broken Willow – then gave the Morning Swim an hour before finishing up in the Vole Pitch.' Some names are self-explanatory: the Goose-shit Swim requires little further description. Whereas many spots are titled eponymously, such as Parr's Pool. From where I am standing now, I can see Ellie's Swim, Martin's Swim and, in the distance, the tall reeds that line Spence's Bend.

All have changed markedly since being named, but all at some stage were prime perch swims. Perch, being a short-lived species, tend to boom and bust. A couple of good year classes will coincide with a glut of prey, such as minnows, and go on to grow fast and fat. But those fish will all die at a similar time and a stretch of water that was full of big perch one winter may seem all but empty the next.

In the days when I came here often, I would always be confident of finding some perch around Parr's Pool, even though, as with other swims, its character has changed considerably in the past decade. Being sheltered and steady, this tiny carrier is a magnet for fry and minnows. The sedge is too thick for herons and kingfishers to beak their way through; and while the bigger predatory fish – pike, trout and chub – might work their way up here, they become easy prey for the local otters when they do. This leaves the perch to dominate the food chain in this small microcosm of Kennet life. The fish's compact form allows it to squeeze tight against the sedge stems and its stripes keep it camouflaged like a tiger in long grass.

Although sedges run the length of this carrier, they are particularly dense around Parr's Pool. The water widens very slightly here too, while a ridge pushes up under one side, thick with liverwort and nudging the water across the stream. Over time, and when the current has stiffened, a hole has been bored out from the near side. This in itself is a notable feature in such a tight, narrow environment, and once a fallen branch from a nearby alder even gave it a roof. The branch itself wasn't thick, but collected dead stems and loose weed that trailed behind it like contrails from an aircraft's wing. The perch would cram in underneath, never wanting to move upstream of the branch, but always ready to intercept any morsels that might drift past.

It was tricky to fish, though. Any movement too near the hotspot would see the fish flee, so I would position myself ten or twelve yards upstream. A ledgered bait was the obvious tactic, but the bottom was crawling with signal crayfish that would shred a bait within seconds. Instead, I would let a float work down to the branch and then tighten up to it. The current would draw the float across to the left-hand side and lift the bait (a worm) up underneath. Bites were normally immediate, and the float would donk as the perch engulfed the bait before slipping away.

With a steady trickle of bait, and regular breaks for the perch to regain their confidence, some fabulous fishing could be had. My best afternoon saw me take nineteen perch weighing up to nearly three pounds, with a couple of nice chub adding to the excitement. The fight would be incredible in such tight confines, and the intimacy made the experience even more intense.

As Sue became increasingly ill, and the pressures of work and dwindling finances mounted, this was exactly the place I needed to escape to. I would pop out during my lunch breaks and gather worms; then arrive beside the river just as dawn was smudging up in the east. Time, which for much of the week was a wretched burden, slowed with the rise and fall of my chest. There was no great rush and no pressure. I would put up a rod at my own pace and then walk the meadows. I wouldn't spend all of my time at Parr's Pool, although I would always have a cast or two here, and, as the daylight faded to pink and grey and the lights of the train carriages flickered behind the trees, I would make for home with a mind uncluttered.

| |

SLOWING DOWN

The Stour

It is mid-morning but the grass still glistens with last evening's dew. The ash keys are browning and the combine harvesters have been busy in the fields. There is time yet for summer to have a blast, but today it feels as though the world is drifting drowsily into autumn.

It is a bittersweet time of year. A flush of rain and a drop in temperature will freshen up our rivers, and as the weed dies back and the invertebrate life begins to dwindle, the fish are stirred to feed, perhaps sensing the tough months ahead. It is a good time to be an angler. The fish are often at their finest and the pink evenings are soft yet expectant.

As a child, however, for me late summer meant a new school year and the prospect of life getting that little bit more serious. In July, the holidays seemed to stretch out before me like untrodden sand along a beach. There was no end to this new world, just a wealth of unspoilt opportunity. I would go to bed before the sun and my skin would glow against cotton sheets. But time slipped away all too fast – the swallows gathered and the fields burned – and a soft morning such as this would find me wrestling with my school tie as I waited for the bus.

This summer has been particularly changeable. Although not especially wet, the wind has been unrelenting and frequently carrying a northern bite. As good a time as this is for fishing, I am also drawn to the woods. The quiet of the trees, broken only by the babble of a nuthatch or the low drone of a hornet. I creep with my basket and fill it with fungi, returning home to lay out the drying trays and filling jars for winter soups and stews. I am normally ready for autumn – excited about it – but I don't want to let go of summer just yet, and it seems as though the river feels the same way.

The lilies in the pool below me have not even begun to curl, while the rushes around the water's edge still hold a rich, deep green. The water itself is almost at a standstill, as it often is at this time of year, but it doesn't look as though it wants to go anywhere. Often, in summer, the Dorset Stour begins to develop a green tinge. An algal bloom that thickens the water like soup before being diluted by the autumn rain. Yet the river today, while not clear, is looking *thin*. There is still much that should flourish within it before autumn – more microorganisms need to multiply and more insects need to hatch. And it is as if the river knows this. It is dawdling. Hanging on to every weed stem or trailing branch. Perhaps it knows that a huge high pressure system is building, bringing warm air from southern Europe and letting the landscape stand still for a time. The swallows will break from their African push, and gatekeeper butterflies will swarm across the brambles. The river will breathe from surface to bed and hold back while life burgeons within it. Then, when the rains of autumn do finally arrive, they will be welcome.

I'm going to head downstream. I spend barely any time on the Stour in the summer, preferring instead to wait until the flow builds and the weed and reeds retreat. The view from this bridge is of a pool that in winter is big and stirring – relative to the size of the river this far upstream. A twenty-minute walk will take me to another bridge, beneath which the main channel narrows and shallows, and there I will always find some sparkle. Today, I decide to resist the temptation to walk the riverbank – there are too many distractions, although the old railway line makes for a pleasant stroll.

My father has always spoken of his fondness for this stretch of railway. The Dorset Central Railway was regarded by some as a slow and dirty line, but its pace was part of the charm. To eyes that were receptive, the varying landscapes of the Stour valley were more than

177

compensation for the steady progress, and the railway and river were rarely out of sight of one another. Although the Dorset Central was lost, along with so many miles of railway, beneath the axe of Dr Beeching in 1966, parts of the route – such as this stretch – can still be enjoyed on foot. If I were to follow this path to the north, it would soon sweep west and pass close by the Mill at Fiddleford where I fished with Ian Murray those many years ago. I have not returned to Fiddleford – yet at least – though I have explored the Stour for some miles further upstream.

When Sue and I first moved to Dorset, I had hopes of finding untapped fishing on one of the local rivers. While there was the opportunity to cast a fly for brown trout close to our new home, I still hankered for the small-stream perch fishing that I had enjoyed on the Upper Kennet. It felt as though there was a chapter of my fishing life that I needed to complete, even though my 'other' life had changed so completely. Parr's Pool lay a hundred miles away now, though, far beyond reach, but it didn't take long for the slower pace of life to begin to adjust my attitude.

When I was a young man, depression stripped me naked emotionally. When I reached the very bottom of the black pool I had no barriers and no defence – I was utterly exposed. And although I was too ill to worry about how people might see or judge me, I finally began to understand myself. Now that Sue and I were materially bankrupt, we started to realise how wonderfully straightforward life could be. We had no credit, and no means of getting credit. If we wanted to go somewhere or do something we couldn't say sod it and find the money later; we simply couldn't do whatever it was. We had collected plenty of nice 'things' from when we could afford them, and we were, and remain, in a far more comfortable position than many. Yet our material possessions could no longer be readily replaced. Holes in socks would have to be darned and a packet of hooks would need to last ... well, indefinitely.

Our lives have eased as a result, though, and we will take pleasure in such simple things: a cup of tea in the sunshine or a full moon rising above the ridge opposite our cottage. Sometimes perspective is a very lovely thing.

— ◆ —

The path is beginning to open up, and the breeze is working through the beeches on my left, reminding me once more of those great trees at Stourhead. The sound and tone are softer, though – the green of the leaves nudging rather than rustling. A sea still soothed by a high summer sun, yet to build to an autumn roar.

Then, a movement catches my eye. A rabbit? No, that was no rabbit. I smile; I cannot recall seeing a hare before in these fields but I am certain that one just flashed across the path ahead. I quicken my pace before slowing as I reach the gateway. It takes me a minute to find him – a smudge of brown just showing above the grass. If this were an arable field I might have struggled to spot him. Even if the crop had been cut, his colour would have merged into the bare soil and stubble. He looked to be a young animal in the way he moved. His back legs seemed long for his body and almost a little too powerful. As he crossed the soft ground of the path his hind feet slipped and splayed like a speedway rider pushing his luck. He won't be one of this year's leverets, but is likely a young male looking to make his mark in the world. A teenager joyriding in broad daylight, but not really sure who he is trying to impress.

Perhaps sensing my gaze he presses more tightly into the grass. I will leave him be, and work my way back down to the river. I am curious to see how it will look below this next bridge. It is a pool I have fished many times but I have never glimpsed it this early in the season.

The Dorset Stour is a river with a rich fishing heritage and the lower reaches are particularly noted. Stretches at Throop and Parley attract anglers from across the country, with massive chub and barbel the most popular targets. In times past, it was renowned for the quality of its roach, and for many years held the British record. Today, while roach are still present throughout the river, the big fish are few and far between. Although this could be cyclical, it is a trend that dates back almost to the capture of that record fish of four pounds three ounces in 1990. Many anglers blame the winter flocks of cormorants and the increasingly active otter population. There will be some truth to this, but as is the case in the nearby Hampshire

Avon, a greater presence of predators does not necessarily correlate with a reduction in number of prey species. A river is such a delicate environment that subtle differences in water quality and climate can have a huge impact upon the natural balance.

That said, otter numbers have certainly increased over the last half century, but more pertinent is their change of habit. These days they are often sighted during the daylight hours, whereas not so many years ago, they were usually only spotted at night. Having long been persecuted by humans, otters became secretive and mostly nocturnal. Glimpses of them would be fleeting and often the only signs of their presence were droppings on the riverbank or the occasional swirl in the water. Adding to this was the fact that the otter's favourite prey fish, the eel, is most active after dark.

The contrast in fortunes of the eel and otter over the past few decades could not be greater. The eel is in massive decline, with estimates suggesting a crash in population of up to 99 per cent across Europe. Blighted by a parasitic nematode worm that arrived from the Far East, the curious breeding cycle of the eel has also caused issue. All of our freshwater eels are believed to migrate to the Sargasso Sea in order to breed, with the resulting fry, unable to swim for themselves, carried back across the Atlantic on tidal currents. With a fluctuating Gulf Stream, the tiny elvers often miss their target, and instead of finding the estuaries of Western Europe, disappear into the icy oblivion of the Arctic. Although numbers over the last few years have recovered slightly, the long-term impact is uncertain, and a fish that was once maligned by anglers for being a slimy, tackle-tangling menace is now all too rarely caught.

While our riverbeds no longer come alive with eels after dark, the change of the otter's routine cannot simply be attributed to the eel's demise. With successive generations of otter being born into a world where humans no longer present such a threat, the instinct of fear is being bred out of them. While an otter is not likely to slip from the water and curl up beneath my feet, they have swum and hunted within a few yards of where I have fished and have seemed completely oblivious to my presence.

Further downstream on the Stour, in the towns of Blandford and Wimbourne, the otters have become local attractions, and people visit daily to take photographs and watch them. Being so visible, it is easy to assume that they are more widespread than they actually are, but in reality, though there are likely more otters in Britain than ever before, it is a population that is self-regulating. Dog otters are highly territorial and will attack and kill young males encroaching on their piece of river. The problem is, though, while otters can balance a lack of fish prey by feasting on signal crayfish or swan mussels, they will return to the same shoal or location to find a meal. The bigger fish, those prized by anglers, are the easiest and most efficient captures and an otter will comfortably take a twenty-pound carp. Having killed the fish they will generally take just one meal from it – normally eating the rich meat around the gills and leaving the remainder to be scavenged. Over a short period of time a localised population of fish can be decimated by an otter feeding in this way. And while, in time, a balance will return, it may not tip in the direction it once did. So, just as I recently lamented the Kennet, anglers will continue to mourn the loss of what once was.

— 🐟 —

For about ten minutes it felt as if the sky might clear. I could feel the sun against my skin and the damp ground began to steam. But instead of clearing, the cloud merely seems to have lifted a few thousand feet and regrouped, leaving a day that errs closer to overcast than hazy. The fish beneath the bridge don't mind a jot, though. The shallow, pacey water is thick with dace that dance in the oxygen-rich current. There is normally a noticeable movement of water here, as the river straightens out from a deep horseshoe bend and cuts across a thin gravel bed. Now, however, just above the bridge, a fallen ash tree lies across the outside of the bend, channelling more water across the shallows.

For twenty yards or so the Stour moves with a fresh purpose. For the previous mile or so, the river has not been a river at all, but more like a succession of ponds – separated by reed beds and lily pads. Any flow has been negligible and certainly not very visible. If the wind were stiff and southerly, the movement on the water's surface would negate any push that came from beneath.

Here, though, for few swipes of a salmon's tail, the Stour is a spritely little stream – flowing fast and clear. I could be forgiven for thinking I am peering into the Kennet or the Avon, whereas if I turn around and look upstream I see only the dark sluggish mystery of a summer Mole, shrinking back from the light. This has always been a favourite spot of mine to fish, and the first fish I ever saw on the bank of this stretch was caught from this pool. Not that it came to my rod.

I was fishing as a guest of Chris's, and it was the first time I had ever even looked at this part of the river. We had fished together further downstream, and Chris had spoken much of this particular stretch, but I have to admit, I wasn't instantly enamoured of it. Before I had a cast, I watched Chris run a float down the tail of this pool to where the water slowed and deepened beneath the trailing branches of a willow. He was hoping for a perch, but instead hooked a beautiful roach of perhaps a pound and a half. It glistened in the low sun – as much gold as silver – and I fully expected to catch one equally handsome. Instead, I missed bites, tangled my line and lost my favourite float in a weed bed. Then, having finally hooked a fish – a decent chub – the hook hold gave as it dived for cover and my rod tip sprang back and cracked against a branch above me. I fished on with a shortened rod but didn't catch a thing, and the pool we finished up in was positively sinister – complete with the pale white face of a man staring at me from the bushes on the far bank. (I never discovered who it was.)

I limped home that night, licking my wounds and wondering quite how I had offended the river so badly. As it transpired, it underlined a peculiar relationship with the River Stour that has endured to this day.

— ◄ —

A chalk stream is fairly predictable. Unless rainfall is extreme, it will rise with the water table, not of its own volition. The colour and water temperature, although not constant, are certainly consistent, especially in the upper reaches of the stream. Changes in conditions are gradual and often quite subtle, allowing life within the river to adjust accordingly.

The Stour, on the other hand, behaves with an erratic immediacy. I have sat beside it and watched it change colour in minutes. A wellington boot that was kissing the margin on arrival can be ankle deep within an hour. And though the fish here will be slightly more adaptable than their chalk-stream cousins, they are still acutely sensitive to the environment in which they live. The Stour can slip into slumber for weeks on end; then, just when you begin to suspect that there are no fish left in the river, the water warms by half a degree and you get a bite after every cast.

My own relationship with the Stour runs even more deeply than the fishing, though, and I wonder if this might be a reflection of myself as an angler. Ever since Sue and I moved to Dorset and stripped our lives back, I have become more deeply immersed in the world around me. We have little choice but to make the most of living locally, but with so much wealth on our doorstep this is no hardship. In the wooded valley beneath the cottage, where buzzards nest and roe deer tiptoe, is a lake full of carp. There are kingfishers, grass snakes and dragonflies. Swallows and martins fill the summer sky while bats and badgers play after dark. And although we no longer own a house, when the sun streams through the windows of our rented home in the morning, where so much changes outside each single night, it simply doesn't matter.

I used to fish to escape reality. In those days, I was driven by the need to catch increasingly bigger and better fish – a desire that gave me something to cling to until I next set foot on the riverbank. Now, though, fishing complements my life. It is a luxury of sorts, and while I still want to catch fish, far more important is the connection I feel with the river itself. I seem more sensitive to the natural world, and although I am no woodsman who knows every twig, nor a sailor with salt in his bones, my mood definitely shifts with the natural rhythm of things.

This new awareness is something that's difficult to quantify and almost impossible to be aware of in the moment. Rather like those seconds between consciousness and sleep, when your mind begins to drift: if you think too hard then you snap yourself awake. But this sense of harmony with my surroundings has become even more profound over the last few years. I no longer fret about delivery rotas or shipping costs and instead find myself troubled by the late showing of the local adders or a lack of nettles for the small tortoiseshells and peacocks.

— ⋆ —

A loud splash catches my attention. Ripples are rolling out from the slack water beneath the willows. It can only have been a pike, and the scatter of minnows a few seconds later confirms it. The otters on this stretch have not become as diurnally active as they have elsewhere on the river, though the empty mussel shells in the shallows to my right is ample evidence of the mammal's presence. That swirl was definitely fishy and, knowing that this is a popular spot for pike to lay up in, I have no doubt about its origin.

There are good numbers of pike through this section of river. Jason, who looks after the stretch, has regularly caught fish over twenty pounds, while another friend, Matt, occasionally pops down with a lure rod and has taken a dozen in a single afternoon. But I have never felt drawn towards pike angling. They are amazing fish – built for short bursts of extraordinary speed as they break hours of inactivity with a sudden lunge and toothy grab. Yet, despite a ferocious appearance, pike are delicate creatures. They have evolved little since the last Ice Age, and have no need to, but their basic biology leaves them vulnerable. They should be handled with care and not just because they are susceptible to damage – they can inflict some nasty damage on their captor. A pike's teeth are razor sharp and many, perfect for grabbing prey. They are also coated in an anticoagulant that can leave the tiniest nick bleeding for hours. A pike angler's tackle box, while containing all manner of tools to enable safe unhooking, will likely house a first aid kit, or at least a packet of sticking plasters.

Though I do not fish for them, I nevertheless hook plenty of pike. They will often grab a worm intended for perch, or snaffle a small fish as you reel it in. The pike that swirled the water here is likely one I have encountered before. It is rare that I fish this stretch of river without at least a couple of casts into this swim, and it is then unusual not to have at least one close shave with a pike.

The pike is a fish of habit, and can often be found occupying the same lie. When not driven by the urge to spawn, they are solitary creatures – and the smaller male fish, known as jacks, will do well to keep away from the bigger females, the jills, for fear of becoming lunch. All fish will vary in colour from river to river depending upon the water clarity, and pike are no different. In the clear water of a chalk stream or Scottish loch, they look freshly painted. The deep juniper-green on the back softens to lime along the flank before reaching the white of the belly.

While, in these conditions, the yellow spots that dot the sides of the fish are so sharp they look like buttercups in a spring meadow. The pattern makes for surprisingly good camouflage. From above, the mottling dissolves the pike's form, smudging into the yellows and golds of the gravel beneath. In more coloured water, old estate lakes or silted rivers, the green of the back darkens to almost black and even the biggest females can skulk unnoticed in the shadows.

On Alresford Pond, in central Hampshire, where I spent much of my childhood fishing, I knew a few spots where the same pike always seemed to be lying. The fishing was often slow, and it would bolster my spirits to actually see a few fish. One jack of four or five pounds would invariably be below a broken willow tree, in a spot that required a bit of light-footed dexterity to reach. On one occasion, having inched out along the branch to the jack's lair, I couldn't make him out. The sun was quite high and I guessed that he might be lower in the water, so I leaned in for a closer look. My nose was almost touching the surface when my eyes finally adjusted. He wasn't there – but *she* was. A great big female, at least twenty-five pounds and probably more. She was only an inch or two beneath the surface but, having expected to see a fish substantially smaller, I had looked straight through her. The next few seconds were a blur. I jumped, recoiled and my movement caused the pike to explode. I nearly went in, and one foot slipped, but I managed to hang on to the branch beside me and swing round like a chimpanzee on a vine. The splash was immense, leaving me sodden, though the sound seemed to come long after the actual moment. When it came it did so in stages, as if my mind were retrospectively putting the pieces together.

I had a similar sensation fifteen years ago, when somebody smashed a glass in my face. A late walk home had led us into a gang of over-excited adolescents, intent on trouble. We ran, but I was cornered behind some parked cars and my unashamed pleading came to nothing. I saw the glass coming and time slowed, my ears closing with my eyes. There was no noise, though it came moments later – distorted by my imagination. A tumbling, almost soothing, glass cascade, borrowed from a film rather than based upon reality.

The pike splash that day was the same. I heard all the droplets of water falling around me – not like rain but like a fizzing shower of glitter. On both occasions, my senses reacted in order of importance: each incident posed a threat, but in the moment my mind blocked out the sound so as to not clutter my sight and my clarity of thought. When my mind searched for the accompanying soundtrack all it could find was an associated memory.

— 🐟 —

I have dropped a short distance below the bridge and am sitting beside the foot of an alder. There is a short line of trees on this bank. All are mature and all have the spider-leg root structure that the fish of the Little Weir on the Kennet found so irresistible. The water is shallow and slow beneath this bank, though, and despite the roots, the fish are normally found further across towards the willows on the far bank. The central channel drops away and the current slows, in contrast to the bubbling riffles beneath the bridge. There is good water here – well oxygenated but without an energy-sapping flow to work against.

This is actually the swim where I broke my rod tip on my first visit here, though I have buried the ghost of that day since. In fact, I fished here in the final day of last season, float fishing with a light line and a steady trickle of maggots. It was lovely, fun fishing, with a shoal of chunky roach vying for the bait with dace, a smatter of small chub and some glorious gudgeon. I enjoyed every moment, and didn't care about the size of the fish I was catching. There are other stretches of the Stour that I visit to target bigger fish, particularly perch, but the monster barbel and chub that lurk in the lower reaches can wait for now. I am content to cast upstream for a good while yet.

12

NEW BEGINNINGS

The Sea

The sea is lively this morning. Stirred up by a stiff southerly wind, big waves crash angrily into the pebbles, dragging them screeching into the water only to slap them straight back up the beach again. Rain is coming – squally showers that are due to precede something more persistent. I had hoped to complete some kind of circle today. Recalling the noise of the wind in the beech trees at Stourhead, I was looking forward to sitting on the shingle, closing my eyes and pretending I was back there once more. But, unless I'd like to imagine whole limbs being wrenched from tree trunks, the similarity of sound is a long way off.

The weather is quite a contrast too. I wore my shorts and flip-flops at Stourhead, eleven months ago, and today I've got a woollen hat on. I quite like it. Knowing the car is only a short sprint away and home just a few miles inland, I will stay while the rain remains light. I haven't brought a rod with me, as I knew the sea would be unfishable. A couple of hardy souls are pitched up further down the beach, but they are huddled into little canvas shelters while their rods sit redundant, and they wait hoping for a change in the weather or at least a break from the breeze. They remain resolute, and are seemingly more content to be sitting beside an almost unfishable sea than anywhere else. They likely have saltwater in their souls.

While my relationship with the sea is still in its infancy, many of those who have lived beside it, particularly through their formative years, maintain a relationship with the water that is profound. It is such an immense thing, the sea. Not only in physical size but in comprehension and influence. A human life seems insignificant beside it, but rather than this leading to a sense of irrelevance, one can actually gain perspective from it. A trivial issue that niggles and becomes compounded within the confines of four walls can be snuffed out by a single blast of salty air. And, although nobody should ever consider themselves or their troubles unimportant, the opportunity to reflect within a fresh context can offer a degree of objectivity.

A lone herring gull rides the wind from right to left – west to east. It keeps fairly low over the waves but does not seem to be looking for food. Gulls ride the wind effortlessly, although it is an obstacle with which they must contend from the moment they fledge. They have a frame like a glider, with long, stiff wings that cut through the air without being buffeted. In some towns, particularly those beside the sea, gulls are viewed with disdain – their food-pinching prowess leading to encounters far too close for many people's liking. Sadly, this is a problem of our own making. Not just as a result of our feeding them directly, but an association for gulls of humans with food that goes back centuries. Fishing boats are always worth following, as the steady stream of by-catch and fish guts will testify. There are more opportunities back in the harbour, as decks are cleaned and pots baited. For many years the relationship has worked both ways. The gulls clean up after the fishermen and get lunch into the bargain.

Humankind's propensity to litter and waste food, though, has exacerbated the problem, particularly as fishing catches have dwindled. Gulls have been forced to become less fearful, yet wherever we go we leave food for them. Late-night takeaways end up in gutters, plastic bags bulge beside bins that are already full. In Britain we throw away more than 300,000 tons of bread each year – while we cast scorn on the gulls that are feasting on our mess.

I rather like the birds. They come in all sorts of shapes and sizes, from the diminutive little gull, which is smaller than a jackdaw, to the great black-backed, which sports a wingspan approaching five and a half feet. In summer plumage, adult gulls look smart, and with so many species in decline perhaps we should pay them a little more respect.

The gulls along Chesil are used to the anglers and, whereas last year I looked to the birds for clues about the presence of fish, here, where the beach is considerably busier, our roles are reversed. It could be that the gulls are deterred by the activity over the water, but more likely they are being opportunistic. They watch for whoever is catching and wait beside them. The smaller mackerel will be tossed back into the surf, while some anglers gut and clean the fish as they unhook them. Those anglers using bait will normally leave what they don't use and rinse their bait buckets in the surf. Plenty of scraps for little effort.

I am sure that even on a busy beach the gulls would react to a fish frenzy. Normally, the small bait fish – whitebait or sand eels – are chased into shore by the mackerel and scad. The bait fish will scatter in an explosion of silver, often within feet of the beach, as the bigger fish plough into them. It isn't just the gulls that join in the feast, though. As I witnessed last summer, the local crows are wise to the event.

On that day, my first fishing trip to Chesil, the sea was alive. Although I was unaware of it at the time, that particular shoreline is considerably shallower than elsewhere along this coast. After days of hot sun and calm seas, the bait fish had been drawn into the warm shallow water and the mackerel shoals were not far behind. As the tide started to flood, so the fish moved with it and the sea began to boil. My first cast, with four feathers, produced four mackerel, and I foolishly thought that mackerel fishing from the beach would always be this easy. The most amazing spectacle that day, though, was the tens of thousands of dead and dying fish being nudged up the beach with the tide. As I looked to either side of where I sat, it seemed as though the sea was edged in silver, and the crows and gulls gorged until they could eat no more. It was difficult to comprehend just how many millions of these tiny whitebait there were in the water before me. And all along the shore the sea boiled as shoal after shoal of mackerel scattered them skyward. There were bigger swirls too, as the bass began to stir. They wouldn't worry about the tiny silver flashes but would be taking the mackerel themselves, and I tied on a single, big lure in the hope of fooling one. Getting anything through the mackerel was impossible, though. As soon as the lure hit the water it was grabbed or tugged. As I reeled in another fish something substantial snaffled it, and the rod wrenched over. For three or four seconds the clutch of the reel whirred as the bass – it was surely a bass – took line, but then the rod tip sprang straight and I was left without either fish.

As the last Ice Age ended, and sea levels began to rise, a series of sandy deposits across Lyme Bay were eroded and the resulting particles washed inshore where they began to collect and form a ridge parallel with the land. As the gravel and sand deposits built, and the sea level continued to drop, the ridge became a barrier – impenetrable to the highest of tides. Today, Chesil Beach measures eighteen miles long and between Ferrybridge and Abbotsbury it takes the form of a narrow strip dividing the sea and Fleet Lagoon – a shallow, brackish stretch of water that is linked to the sea via a narrow channel at its eastern end. The lagoon is tidal and rich in invertebrate life, providing a perfect nursery ground for young bass and mullet. It has a curious atmosphere. From the northern bank, it has the appearance of a great mere, only with seaweed instead of lily pads and with a distinctly salty edge. It is hard to believe that the sea rolls just beyond the great shingle bank that forms the seaward shore.

Sue and I honeymooned close to the Fleet, during an erratic spring. Our wedding took place the only settled day among a steady roll of Atlantic storms. We stayed in a cosy cottage with an open fire, pulled the sofa up to the hearth and bedded in. I found a dog-eared copy of J. Meade Falkner's novel *Moonfleet* on one of the bookshelves and it was a tale that held great resonance for me, considering our location. The exposed centre beam in the cottage was made from the salvaged mast of a wrecked ship – in common with many of the properties in the area. Though treated and shaped for its new purpose, it still bore the notches and scars delivered by the merciless sea.

The unique form of Chesil Beach plays a prominent role within Falkner's novel. The sea is a constant presence, and the lives of the local residents are linked intrinsically with it. As a storm builds the children sing, '*Blow wind rise storm, Ship ashore before morn,*' not quite trivialising an inevitable shipwreck, but certainly emphasising the normality of it. Even without a big tide, a vicious undertow is formed against the steep beach. When the sea is rough, like today, it is unforgiving. Inshore wrecks are dotted all along Chesil, and only this summer a man lost his life along here, having saved that of his young son.

In *Moonfleet*, Falkner mentions a 'back-suck of pebbles' that can be heard as far inland as the town of Dorchester. As the wind settles after a storm, the sea is quick to reshape the beach. It is a sound I have not heard, although there is enough noise today to imagine that on a clear night it might echo through my dreams.

Two winters ago there were a series of brutal weather systems that caused flooding across Britain and twisted the contours of Chesil Beach. Spring tides combined with torrential rain and gale-force winds to lift thousands of tons of stone and drop it fifty yards inland. After the most tempestuous night at home, I came down to survey the scene. I was unable to walk far – the path that runs behind the beach had disappeared beneath several feet of pebbles, and walking over the loose stones was like wading through treacle. Dead seabirds littered the ground, mainly razorbills and guillemots, but also a rarer black guillemot and a puffin. All birds that spend the winter on the open sea. It was a scene that was repeated all along the south coast. Quite how many birds perished and whether this was as a direct result of the weather or an inability to feed in the rough seas will never wholly be known.

That day, when I came down to see the wreckage, it was odd to see the back of the beach look so barren. Normally, the gravel on the inland slope is carpeted with hardy plants such as sea kale, sea beet and thrift. Through the warmer months, the plants spread across the stones, low and compact to withstand the buffeting wind. Although many of them die back in winter, their tight skeletal remains trap food items and offer sanctuary for insects, in turn attracting small birds such as linnets and pipits.

These days, the shape of the beach has settled, with a helping hand from mankind and nature's own remodelling. The plants have found their way skyward and once more form an almost constant band of green along the back of the ridge. This particular stretch of Chesil lies west of the Fleet, and the area between the stones and the exploitable land is a fantastic habitat. These links are thick with scrub, a tangle of hawthorn and blackthorn, restricted by the wind but forming an almost impenetrable mass as a result. There is shelter for all manner of birds and animals, and little interference from humans. Some of the links are grazed but the ground is unsuitable for arable crops – and Nature thrives on nothing like it does on so-called neglect.

It is a vital environment for the adder – a reptile that has been squeezed out of much of its traditional range. Populations have become isolated from one another as more land has been turned over to agricultural use and will dwindle further in the face of the resulting inbreeding and diminished habitat. As I look back inland to the slopes that rise up to the hedgerows and fields of the ridgeway, there is alarmingly little depth to the dry scrub that adders require. Yet a glance east and west is far more promising. The thin strip of inhabitable territory picks a path for many miles and here and there it fingers its way inland, into dry valleys or over rocky outcrops, allowing a thinly stretched head of snakes to slither with space to spare.

The sea has definitely calmed. Not enough to tempt me to cast (not that I have a rod with me) but enough to coax a few more gulls into the air. A small group of gulls has settled on the water about a hundred yards offshore, appearing and disappearing as they ride the swell. I scan through them to check for any Mediterranean gulls, but all are the more familiar black-headed. Rather like the little egret, the Mediterranean gull is a bird that has only recently colonised Britain. When I was a teenager, one appeared at Alresford Pond and caused a minor sensation. I arrived one morning to fish and found a small army of birders with their telescopes trained. The birds are similar in size and appearance to black-headed gulls but look sharper with blood-red legs and bill and all-white wings.

As I scan to find one without success, I do pick up a much bigger bird further out to sea. A gannet moves west to east with its rather languid wing beat. I watch as it pauses and circles, but it doesn't dive. They are big birds, with a wingspan of over six feet, and have the ability to fold their wings behind them and dive beak first, hitting the water at up to sixty miles per hour. This bird would almost certainly be from the colony that nest just off Alderney in the Channel Islands. A gannet may benefit from the safety of living in numbers, but it does require a long trip to find its dinner.

The day is changing. The wind has dropped to a loud whisper and the sea has responded: the waves roll rather than crash, as if waiting in anticipation. The black-headed gulls rise from the swell and swing back onto the beach, settling near the top of the ridge to my right. As I watch them, I notice the sky blackening further to the west. The cloud is unbroken overhead, but a weather front is coming and it is bringing rain. Rain is already sheeting down across towards Lyme Regis and it cuts a line out to the horizon. I'll wait here for a few moments, but as soon as the downpour reaches Golden Cap, the highest point along the entire South Coast, I'll slip back to the car.

I always find it disconcerting to look at the sea and imagine how it would appear without any water. The seabed here drops away quite sharply, although there is a trough that runs parallel with the beach about a hundred yards offshore at low tide. A former neighbour used to dive extensively along this coast and spoke of the huge bass that he swam beside as he worked his way along the gully. The seabed there was a graveyard of lost fishing weights, lumps of metal and waterlogged wood, he said. And in between the debris, crabs scuttled and small fish skitted, scavenging for scraps while trying to avoid the great gape of the bass above.

I have looked hard for signs of that trough – expecting the water to break slightly differently as it moves above it. As yet, I haven't seen any anomaly that might give its presence away. It could be that the gully is too subtle a feature to affect any movement on the surface, but it is more likely that I have still to learn the subtleties of the sea here. And I had also hoped to have fished an evening or two this summer and to find the bass crashing into the mackerel once again. The autumn may yet bring opportunity, but it looks increasingly likely that I shall wait until next year.

My friend Matt, who does so well with the pike on the Stour, has caught some incredible bass along this coast. He is canny as to exactly where (though I know it is not here), but was happy for me to join him on the waves for a couple of hours last summer. I didn't last long on his boat, looking away from the water as a big wave walloped us and instantly losing my sea legs.

The wind is picking up again now, but no longer from the south. The rain clouds are chasing it from the west, and for the first time today I can hear it rattling through the great reed bed that runs along the back of the beach. The reed stems are dry and browned, the seed heads largely spent. As they clatter into one another the sound is hard and almost like fabric, like the thump of a foresail being hauled up the mast.

Back in early June, when we came here to celebrate Sue's birthday, the sound from the reeds was a very different chatter. Reed, sedge and Cetti's warblers, whitethroats, stonechats and reed buntings were all tchakking and chirring. I stood on the edge of the reed bed and closed my eyes and cupped my ears. It was impossible to sift out the individual songs, and with my eyes open there was not a single feather to be seen. The breeze was stiff that day too, and though they sang loudly the birds did so from deep within the stems.

The storms of two winters past would likely have changed the balance of this wetland. Despite its proximity to the sea, the water beneath the reeds presents a freshwater environment. It will be high in salinity but is fed from inland, and the reeds filter the water and remove impurities. In the centre of the reed bed is an open area that is busy with wildfowl. Mallards, coots and moorhens in the summer are joined by gadwall, shoveller and teal in the winter. Life within the water itself is hard to gauge. The sediment should be rich enough to support plenty of invertebrate life, and I would imagine fish such as three-spined sticklebacks, which cope well with brackish water, must be present. The only fish I have seen here was a carp. A fish of seven or eight pounds that was nosing around the surface in a small gap in the reeds. I did consider catching it – largely because I wanted to prove to myself what I had seen. It seemed fairly oblivious to my presence and would surely have found a small piece of bread crust irresistible. But if hooking the carp seemed straightforward, landing it would have proved almost impossible: there is no way I could have kept it out of the dense reed stems.

That carp will have done well to survive the saltwater surge that came with those winter storms, but it, and any other fish present, may have become tolerant enough to endure. The adders too will have suffered, though it will be difficult to know to what extent. While I was looking for adders on my local patch in the early spring, I met a lady in her eighties who spoke of her childhood encounters with the snakes along this coast. She recalled seeing balls of battling males that numbered thirty or forty individuals, whereas I have not even witnessed two dancing their post-hibernation duet. They are hanging on still, but only by the tips of their scales.

— 🐟 —

It is time to move. The rain is coming more quickly than I realised. Golden Cap has vanished beneath low cloud and anyone loitering on the quay at West Bay will be getting peppered. The rain is pulsing; spiralling across the sea like the rolls of the waves themselves. It is almost upon me.

I shut the car door and sink into the seat. I am taken back to a day on the Hampshire Avon, when my friend Kieran caught his first and only chub. We dodged a storm as the rain pummelled into the roof of the car, thudding like a Chinook, our eardrums aching as thunder crashed.

It is the wind that carries the rain today and it thumps huge fist-sized splotches of water onto the windscreen and leaves the car rocking on its axles. My ears ring and my sinuses bulge as the air pressure plummets, but within a minute the roar lulls as the front pushes through. The rain still comes but with less intensity and the car windows mist up as the temperature outside falls. I shall wait here for now. I am damp, but only got caught by the opening splatters and I'm not uncomfortable or cold.

Hopefully the anglers on the beach didn't lose their shelters to the wind. With their backs to it, they might not have been aware of the downpour's approach, but, providing they kept their shelters, they should have been quite snug with the rain lashing around them. I have had some lovely moments tucked up under a fishing umbrella, everything to hand as the surface of the river steams, and for once willing the float not to go under. Even better are those times when I am totally unprepared, peering out from beneath a beech tree, or best of all a yew, as an unexpected squall reels past my nose. Time is irrelevant in such a moment, I am at the mercy of the weather, and the sense is one of liberation. On occasions like this, my mind drifts; I watch the raindrops flick off the leaves and the tiny trickles twisting through the dust around my toes. Nothing else matters in those moments – work, money, health; without the constraint of time, life is so wonderfully simple.

I can no longer see the sea through the windscreen. The glass inside is thick with condensation, though the rain has eased enough for me to roll down the windows and let the air blow out the moisture. I'll trundle home shortly, put the kettle on and see how Sue is. She'll be curled up on the sofa and pleased to see me. It's been another bad day for her today, but they are getting fewer.

I've not caught a single fish from the sea this year, although I have fished very little anywhere. Last summer, when the mackerel were dancing and the bass were crashing, I felt as though I was casting exactly where I should be. As though the sea was a place of natural progression. But just as I considered the water that day, with its never-ending cycle of evaporation and precipitation, I realised that the pattern suits me as an angler. I am no longer driven by a single species or a single venue, and while I only fish when opportunity dictates, I am more responsive to each moment. If I have the time, and enough fuel in the car, then on a warm day with a flooding tide I will likely pop down to the sea for a cast. Whereas on a dank, grey, early winter morning I might hanker for a trip to the Stour or perhaps the Kennet. Regardless of where I cast, I will benefit far more from my interaction with the water and the life around it than from whatever I might happen to catch.

I have been invited to fish a new river next month. A place that I have heard much about and where apparently the quality of the fishing is superseded only by the scenery. I am excited by it, and a little nervous. I really don't mind if I catch nothing, but I want the river to accept me. I want to feel connected to it. That way, I will feel part of the trees and the hills and the passage of the valley, and in such a place, the float need never dip.

It'll be nice if it does, though …

GLOSSARY OF ANGLING TERMS

Though this is not a book solely about fishing, I am an angler and sometimes I cannot help but use terms that non-fisherfolk might raise an eyebrow at. This short glossary will hopefully clear up any confusion.

Bait: any item, natural or artificial, that is attached to the **hook** in order to entice a fish into eating it.

Bite: the moment a fish takes a **bait** into its mouth.

Carrier: a small, often man-made, **side stream** designed to take water from the main river in order to irrigate land or power a mill wheel, or ease the volume of water to prevent flooding.

Cast (vb.): the action of 'casting' one's **line**, and baited **hook**, into the water.

Catch on a fly: see **Fly**

Crease: the point where fast and slow moving water meet, creating a 'crease' in the surface.

Float (n.): a slim piece of wood, quill or plastic, with a coloured tip, that is attached to the **line** and used to suspend a **bait** at a specific depth in the water and also as a means of **bite** indication. The float typically 'dips' as a fish takes the bait.

Floating bait: a bait such as bread crust that will float upon the surface and attract fish, typically carp, chub or trout, that are lying in the upper levels on the water.

Flooding tide: see **Tide**.

Fly (n.): an artificial bait, tied onto a hook with different coloured feathers and threads, designed to imitate specific insects that the fish might be feeding upon. A **dry-fly** is designed to float whereas a **wet-fly** sinks. To '**catch on a fly**' is a term often referred to when trout or salmon fishing where the target fish has been fooled with an artificial bait such as that described rather than a **spinner** or **natural bait** that is more effective but requires less skill to use.

Free-lining: a method where only a **hook** is tied to the **line**, which is then baited and 'free-lined' into the water, causing minimal disturbance to the fish.

Glide (n.): a piece of water that is uniform in depth, width and flow, where fish might be swimming. Often apparent by the smooth, almost glassy, surface.

Gold-headed nymph: a type of **nymph**.

Hook (n.): a curved piece of metal that is tied to the end of the **line** and carries the **bait** before 'hooking' in a fish's mouth.

Ledger or Leger: a weight attached to the line in order to sink a **bait** and hold it in place on the bottom of a river- or seabed.

Line: a thin length of 'string', attached to the **rod** via a **reel** to which a **hook** is tied. Traditionally made from horsehair or gut, modern lines are almost all synthetic.

Lure (n.): an artificial bait, such as a **spinner, fly** or **team** of feathers that is used to either imitate a specific fish's food or provoke an instinctive reaction.

Natural bait: a **bait** such as a worm, maggot, or elderberry that the fish may well eat as part of their normal diet.

Nymph: a **wet-fly** tied to imitate a fly in its naiad (larval) form and fished beneath the surface.

Rise a fish (vb.): to make a fish, often a trout, rise to the surface when casting a **dry-fly** or using a **floating bait**.

Reel: also known as a 'winch', this is attached to the **rod** and houses the **line**. A handle is turned in order to 'reel' the line in.

Rod: a length of carbon, fibreglass or wood, shaped like a pole and with small rings placed at intervals through which **line** is threaded.

Setting (of) the hook: see Strike

Shot: small grooved balls of metal (formerly lead) that are pinched onto the line in order to **cock** a **float** or **ledger** a **bait**.

Side stream: a stretch of running water, normally formed naturally, that has separated from the main river before rejoining it further downstream.

Slack (n.): an area of water, often behind an obstruction such as a bridge or tree, which is away from the main current and has little or no flow.

Snag (n.): an unseen, underwater object, such as a rock or shopping trolley, that 'snags' the angler's tackle, often causing the **line** to break.

Spinner: a metal or wooden **lure**, often shaped like a small fish, that is tied to the **line** and 'spins' as it is retrieved.

Strike: the lifting of the rod in response to a **bite** – resulting in the **setting of the hook** within the fish's mouth.

Swim (n.): a specific spot in the river where one can, or one chooses to, fish.

Tag (n.): the moment when a fish bites at a **lure** without fully taking it – the angler feels a 'tag' on the **line**.

Team of feathers: used principally when fishing for mackerel, a series of three or four hooks are tied to the **line**, each hook carrying a feather or reflective plastic that the fish instinctively grab at.

Tide: the movement of seawater in response to the Moon's gravitational pull. The sea rises (a **flooding tide**) and falls (an **ebbing tide**) typically twice a day.

(a) Water: refers to any specific body of water that may be fished. Be it a river, lake or sea.

Wet-fly: see **Fly.**

RESOURCES

When it comes to references, I admit to having a peculiar
memory, which stores up facts and statistics alongside
vivid moments of the past, but which really needs to be
stirred in order to accept anything new. It's a memory that
is handy for pub quizzes and nostalgic reminiscence, but
no good for filling out tax returns or securing positive
reinforcement in an argument.… Of course, even the most
deeply imbedded thread must have been acquired from
somewhere, and a large proportion of the references in
this book required careful checking before being offered
into print. So, with much appreciation, here follows a list
of sources that have helped me along the way – and my
apologies to any I have inadvertently overlooked.

Websites:

archive.org

berkshirehistory.com

boxhillcommunity.com

capabilitybrown.org

icl.ac.uk

information-britain.co.uk

mvgs.org.uk

naturespot.org

newforestnpa.gov.uk

stourvalleyway.co.uk

theperchfishers.org

treesforlife.org

wikipedia.org

wildtrout.org

Books:

Stefan Buczacki, *Fauna Britannica* (Hamlyn, 2002)

Jon Hardey, Humphrey Crick, Chris Wernham, Helen Riley, Brian Etheridge and Des Thompson, *Raptors – A Field Guide for Surveys and Monitoring* (TSO Ltd, 2006)

ACKNOWLEDGEMENTS

Rivers Run only came about after I was the unwitting beneficiary of a conversation between Sue Lascelles and Chris Yates. The notion for the book was Sue's, and Chris, already involved in a project, nudged her in my direction. I am ever grateful to both. Without Sue Lascelles's input, editing and advice, the manuscript would never have made it beyond a few squiggles. Thank you for all you have done, Sue.

Another Sue, my wife, has given me unwavering love and support, and a reason to get out of bed every morning. I have also had wonderful support from my Mum and Dad, brother Rich and sister Cath, along with the rest of my and Sue's family

The title *Rivers Run* was pinched from a song by Karine Polwart – written after the birth of her first child. It is a lovely song, and if my words resonate half as well as Karine's then I shall be a happy chap.

Rider have been a joy to work with – thank you all and special thanks to Helen Pisano for her eagle-eyed copy-editing.

A motley crew of anglers and friends have aided me along the way; in no particular order I would like to thank Ben Fitch, Martin Stevens, Hugh Ortega Breton, Kieran Topping, Dan Kieran, Steve Dance, Lawrence Pointer, Leapy Leigh, Jon Berry, Garrett Fallon, Peter Arlott, Merv Sands, Matt Spence, Jason White, Les Darlington, Fergus Collins and Steve Clark.